SAMUEL   WALTERS

SAMUEL WALTERS,
LIEUTENANT, R.N.

Reproduced, by permission, from a miniature painted on ivory, in the
possession of Mr. Frank Walters Mills.

SAMUEL WALTERS

LIEUTENANT, R.N.

His memoirs, edited, with
an introduction and notes

by

C. NORTHCOTE PARKINSON

LIVERPOOL
UNIVERSITY PRESS

FOR ALLISON

First published 1949 by
Liverpool University Press
4 Cambridge Street
Liverpool L69 7ZU

This edition published 2005

British Library Cataloguing-in-Publication data
A British Library CIP record is available

SBN 0-85323-149-4

Typeset by Koinonia, Bury
Printed and bound in the European Union
by Bell and Bain Ltd, Glasgow

CONTENTS

ILLUSTRATIONS

PREFACE

By the editor

AT the outbreak of war in 1914 the *S.S. Napierian* was outward bound for
the West Indies, having sailed from Liverpool on July 31st. She was a new
ship of 4,000 tons register, completed that year at Glasgow by Messrs.
Napier and Miller and owned by the Leyland Line of Liverpool. She was
a fine ship but had no wireless and remained, therefore, in ignorance of the
war until she reached St. Thomas. This was but the first of her wartime
voyages on that route, voyages which normally took her to New Orleans.
A photograph taken in May, 1915, shows her leaving Celeste Street Wharf
at that port, headed upstream, but with the tugboat pulling on her port
bow so as to turn her down the Mississippi towards the Mexican Gulf, a
hundred and eleven miles away. The photograph shows her still unarmed,
with peacetime paintwork and flour streaks down her side opposite No. 3
hatch. She had no war-paint nor gun until 1916, and no wireless until the
year after that. In the same photograph can be discerned, though not very
easily, the chief officer, Mr. H. H. Neligan. He is standing in the bows,
near where the tugboat's funnel can be seen, he being in charge forward as
the ship leaves the wharf. The scene was to become familiar enough to
him, for the *Napierian* remained on the same route and he remained her
chief officer until the war ended. To be exact, the armistice found her about
to ship horses and mules at Norfolk, Virginia, and enabled her to come
home without them. This ship's visits to New Orleans had been pretty
regular and there Mr. Neligan had made friends ashore; among them Mr.
A. B. Tipping, Manager of the Tulane Infirmary, at whose house he often
dined.

Although provided with this and other medical establishments, New
Orleans was not, at that period, as hygienic a city as it has since, no doubt,
become. Only recently, in fact, had the local authorities realised that the
older properties of the city were mostly infested with rats, and that rats—or
at any rate rats in that quantity—are (for many reasons) undesirable. They
issued stringent regulations which gave many property-owners the alternative
of making their premises rat-proof or of having them demolished. Faced
with this dilemma, the owners of one block of wooden offices—originally

5

occupied by slave merchants—did not hesitate. Demolition, they decided, would be cheaper and demolition accordingly began. It was in full swing when the *Napierian* entered the Mississippi on what proved to be her last wartime visit. So derelict were these rat-haunted premises that the last tenants had not even removed all their gear and with the rubble hurled out there mingled old ledgers and files and nameless litter. One of the workmen, more observant than the rest, noticed that one tattered volume contained drawings of ships. Thinking that it might be of interest to a sailor, he saved the book and took it home. His son, it so happened, was Mr. Tipping's coloured butler, who, listening to the conversation while he waited at table, had gathered that Mr. Neligan, his master's friend, was from the " big English ship" in the river. The book passed from the father to the son, from the butler to Mr. Tipping, and from him to Mr. Neligan, in whose possession it has since remained. Captain Neligan—as he eventually became—was at sea for many years before finally retiring to live at Prescot near Liverpool. He could see from the first page that the manuscript volume, with its illustrations, had been the work of Lieutenant Samuel Walters, R.N., an officer of H.M. Ship *Raisonable* in 1805. He suspected, if only from the artistic skill shown, that this Walters would probably have been a relative of the other Samuel Walters, the Liverpool marine artist. But the manuscript itself, written small in ink now faded, was too much for his eyesight. He showed it to various friends and one picture from it was reproduced in a periodical. He showed it to Liverpool's leading local historian, Mr. A. C. Wardle, who transcribed part of it before being compelled, by eye-strain, to desist. Finally, after a meeting of the Liverpool Nautical Research Society in 1947, Captain Neligan approached the present editor and gained his interest, subsequently allowing him to borrow the manuscript with a view to publication.

That anything should have come of this loan is due, mainly, to Miss Winifred Lee, on whom the work of transcription mostly fell. With the aid of a powerful lens and her great fund of patience, the whole work was reduced to typescript. Its punctuation and spelling were improved somewhat for the sake of lucidity and the work, as revised, is now before the public. Of its value and interest the reader can judge for himself. It is necessary, however, to describe the original manuscript and show in what ways the published version differs from it. The volume consists of some seventy foolscap pages, originally bound in cloth with a leather spine and measuring about 32 by 20 centimetres. The first thirty-five pages are covered on both sides with a faint but legible handwriting, written small and becoming more congested as the story proceeds. Whereas some of the earlier pages contain no more than thirty-eight lines, many of the later run

6

to as many as sixty-five. This difference was occasioned, no doubt, by the diarist's increasing use of his spectacles. It is good paper with an 1808 watermark. Five charts and views are interspersed with the text. The pictures of ships, seven of them, begin with one of the *Raisonable* on the first page, the remainder being grouped together at the end of the text. A last illustration in this group is a view of Rio Janeiro. Reversing the book and beginning at the other end, the reader finds three more pages of text. The middle of the volume includes two more pages in Walters' handwriting, three pages of accounts dated 1841 in a different handwriting, and eleven pages that are blank. The rest of the book is filled with newspaper cuttings, all carefully pasted in. There is not much system in these. The most obviously relevant dates from 1805 and records the sailing of H.M. Ship *Raisonable* from Cawsand Bay. Of the rest one group, mostly from the *Plymouth and Dock Telegraph,* covers the period 1811-1816. The cuttings from these years include such items as an account of the assassination of Spencer Perceval in 1811 and a Plan for the Intended Breakwater at Plymouth. Inconsequent items for 1812-1813 include "Dock. Poem by W.B.", "Poem. Portsea, 1813", the Unitarian Protest, and notices of stage-coach departures, theatrical entertainments and waxworks. Some family interest may attach to the advertisement (Plymouth, 1813) inserted by the young lady, aged 14, seeking employment with a milliner. They are not otherwise very informative. A second group covers the period 1838-1841 and comprises cuttings from American and Canadian news-papers, the *Boston Transcript,* the *Philadelphia Standard,* the *Harrisburg Gazette,* the *Hartford Patriot,* the *Quebec Newspaper,* the *Montreal News,* the *Albany Atlas,* and the *Daily Picayune.* Interest here centres on the one or two items from New Orleans—an illustrated advertisement for Planters' House, an hotel at St. Louis, in 1841, and the proclamation for a day of national mourning, apparently for the death of a President of the United States. A final item, inserted loose, is a ticket for the Southern Hospital Association Bazaar, held at New Orleans on February 18th, 1867.

Of the contents of the volume only the manuscript part is now published and that in an order which differs from the original. Samuel Walters begins his life story in 1805 and continues it chronologically until 1810. He then adds a list of prizes in which the *Raisonable* shared, some verses on his own early life and other verses written on the occasion of his ship being struck by lightning in 1806. There follow some miscellaneous notes and a short account of his experiences in the *Courageux* in 1810; an account which presently lapses into verse. Next, in two columns, are listed, with translations, " Some French and Latin words and Phrases in common use " —fifty or more of each, including " Ex=late, as the Ex-Emperor Bonaparte,

7

&c." Then comes a piece of moralising headed " To be rich is not to be happy ? " and dated " Dartmoor, 3rd May, 1819," a table showing the dimensions and tonnage of the vessels in which Walters served and a brief account, in tabular form, of his services under the Transport Board in 1813-1815. After the pictures of ships comes a recipe for making size (to be used in varnishing drawings or water-colours) dated from Mile End, Poplar, in December, 1815. This is followed, after another picture, by the pages of accounts, signed " H. Rodd " and dated " Quebec, May, 1841." Then comes the page containing what Samuel Walters evidently intended to be the preface to the completed work. Last of all, at the other end of the book, is his short account of his services in the *Argo* from 1798. As there seemed no point in preserving so accidental a sequence, the material is here printed in a more chronological order, with certain items omitted as tedious, and others relegated to an appendix. Apart from this rearrangement and the revised punctuation, the published book faithfully reproduces the manuscript rescued from the New Orleans dust-heap and given to Captain Neligan thirty-one years ago.

Such a manuscript as this presents to its editor a number of problems. How should it be described ? Who was the author and what was his previous and subsequent career ? When did he write it ? How did it come to be at New Orleans in 1918 ? Of these questions the first is easily answered. Although a diary in appearance, the manuscript was obviously written some time after the events it describes. It may well be based—it presumably is based—on a rough diary kept at the time, but it has been revised and perhaps elaborated as well as transcribed. The result might be regarded as half-way between a diary and a book of memoirs. The narrative for 1805-1810 might have been written while Walters was ashore in 1810, but was more probably written between 1815 and 1819; the years from which two of the items are actually dated. Walters was not much ashore during the period 1811-1813 from which the Plymouth newspaper cuttings derive. These were presumably saved for him and pasted in afterwards.

If this then is a book of memoirs, who was the author ? Answering that question has involved the present editor in a great deal of research and correspondence. After inquiries pursued in the Picton Library, the Admiralty Library, Somerset House, Chaucer House, the Public Record Office and the British Museum, letters have been sent to long-suffering people at Plymouth, Barnstaple, Bideford, Ilfracombe, Swansea, Quebec, Ottawa, and Montreal. Members of the Walters' family have been traced and questioned, one of the most helpful proving to be almost a neighbour of the indomitable transcriber herself. Enough, finally, has been discovered

8

to fill in the largest gaps in Samuel Walters' life as told by himself. Between what is known and what he narrates, between family tradition and reasonable conjecture, it is now possible to reconstruct as much of the author's life as is likely to interest the reader of to-day. For the period covered by the memoirs Samuel Walters can tell his own story, but to that has been added an introduction and a sequel, the one covering his family origin and youth and the other showing something of his later life. To this is subjoined some notes on the later generations of his family, and an account of how the manuscript reached New Orleans. Because of these additions it has been thought proper to avoid, in the main title, the word "memoirs" as being scarcely more accurate than " diary " would have been. The title chosen should avert, at least, all suspicion of pretence.

The editor would wish to thank a number of people who have assisted him in various ways. To the late Captain H. H. Neligan—who lived to see the proofs but died before this book was ready to publish—he is indebted for the manuscript and for the queer story of how it came to light. Without the help of Miss Winifred Lee—a valued member of a remarkable group of evening students—the text might never have been transcribed. Without the help and information supplied by his living kinsfolk, little more would be known of Samuel Walters than he tells us of himself. In this connection thanks are particularly due to Mr. Henry H. Walters of Ainsdale, Mr. F. J. Walters of Birkdale, and Mr. Percy R. Walters of Montreal; as also to Mr. J. S. Cushing, Mr. M. Ogden Haskell, and Mr. Frank Walters Mills, all of Montreal. The photographs of Samuel Walters' sword and sea-chest are reproduced with the help and permission of Mr. Frank Walters Mills, to whom these relics have descended. Among many other people who have been helpful, mention must at least be made of such local historians as Mr. A. C. Wardle of Liverpool, Mrs. M. C. S. Cruwys of Cruwys Morchard in Devonshire, and Mr. Mervyn G. Palmer of the Museum at Ilfracombe. To many librarians, and notably Mr. Smith of the Picton Library at Liverpool, Mr. W. Best Harris of the Plymouth Public Library, Colonel G. E. Marquis (Librarian of the Legislature, Province of Quebec), and Miss Dorothy Dixon of the Ottawa Public Library, the editor is deeply indebted. To them and to others, too numerous to name, his thanks are offered.   C. NORTHCOTE PARKINSON.

INTRODUCTION.

THE Walters' family of Ilfracombe is believed to have originated in Pembrokeshire and crossed from there into Devon. This legend is quite possibly true, for the name was certainly known in Wales, both in Pembrokeshire and Carmarthen, and Ilfracombe is a probable place at which a migrant (say, from Swansea) would have landed. It was, incidentally, Sir Richard Walter of Haverfordwest who was the father of the famous Lucy, whose name was coupled with that of the exiled Charles II. This Welsh origin must remain, however, a probability, whereas the former prevalence of the Walters at Ilfracombe is a matter of fact. They were fairly numerous there in the 18th Century, with others of the name at Barnstable, Ashbury, Sutcombe, and West Putford, not far from Bideford. But there is the normal sort of confusion about spelling (Walter and Waters being common variants) and a likelihood that the name, however spelt, was commonly *pronounced* Waters. The parish registers at Ilfracombe record the baptism of six children, offspring of Robert and Anne Walters, between 1783 and 1802—the second child being named Samuel. But that family, although probably related, is not the family with which we are here concerned. For the Walters with which we have to deal were (or rather, became) chapel folk and do not all figure in the parish registers. They appear first in the person of John Walters, supposed to have been born in 1748 and possibly the son of Miles Walters, baptised at Ilfracombe in 1720. John Walters married Mary de Vessaille (pronounced, and sometimes written, Devershall) at Ilfracombe on 5th April, 1773. She was of about his age and of Huguenot stock. Although married in church, they were members, after about 1775, of the Protestant Dissenters of Ilfracombe. This Ilfracombe Meeting had its own baptismal register, now deposited at Somerset House, in which a Catherine Walters, daughter of Thomas and Sarah, his wife, appear as early as 1760. But there is an unfortunate gap in the register from 1771 to 1785. Thereafter the Walters entries include:

Henrietta Walters, Daughter of John and Mary Walters of Ilfracombe, was baptised May 2nd, 1788.—Mr. Shattock.

Elizabeth Walters, Daughter of Sam'l and Elizabeth Walters of Ilfracombe, was born Octob'r 18th, 1803.

Catherine Walters, Daughter of Rob't and Ann Walters of Ilfracombe, was born November 2nd, 1804.

The last two entries relate to the previously Church of England Walters, who evidently experienced conversion in 1803. The first is the only baptism recorded of John Walters' offspring, the other births falling within the period during which the register was apparently neglected. We know, however, from other sources that his family comprised four children, Henrietta being the youngest. These children were:

(1) Miles Walters. Baptised 22nd May, 1774, in the parish church.

(2) Myra Walters. Born circa 1776.

(3) Samuel Walters. Born 10th June, 1778, and

(4) Henrietta Walters. Born (as we have seen) in 1788.

If there were other children (born, e.g., between 1779 and 1785) nothing seems to be known about them. They may have died in infancy.

So far as can be ascertained, John Walters was a builder; or possibly a carpenter and boat-builder. The family was evidently of fairly humble status but respectable and far removed from actual poverty. Samuel, the second son, was the author of the manuscript already described and is henceforward the chief character in the story, in which Miles and Henrietta have also a part to play. Myra Walters disappears temporarily from the scene with her marriage in 1795 to Robert Dyde of London. It is sufficient for the present purpose to note that Robert Dyde migrated to Montreal, Canada, in 1814. He died there in 1818 but Myra Dyde married again in 1824 and continued to flourish until her death in 1866 at the age of ninety. Her eldest son, John Dyde, rose to a position of importance in Canada, partly as manager of the Towboat Company and partly as an officer in the local volunteers of which he eventually became Colonel. This relationship was of great consequence to Samuel and Henrietta in later life.

Of the Walters' life at Ilfracombe relatively little is known. John Walters had kept a sort of commonplace book between 1768 and 1772, containing copies of sermons and hymns dating from the Anglican phase of his religious life and ending shortly before his marriage. This book still exists and is in the possession of his Macdougall descendants of Montreal. Whatever his own trade, it is fairly certain that both his sons were apprenticed as shipwrights; a circumstance which suggests that he may, after 1788, have moved to Bideford. For one thing, legend connects the family with Bideford. What is more, however, to the point is the apprenticeship of his sons. Ilfracombe was all very well as a fishing village and even as a packet station for Bristol, Swansea, and Milford Haven, but it was no place to learn shipbuilding. They made boats there, no doubt. But the nearest shipwrights were at Barnstaple and Bideford where, incidentally, the name of Waters was known in the trade. Is it a coincidence that the first vessels of any size to be built at Bideford, the *Fanny* of 300 tons, and the *William and James* of 264 tons, were actually built in 1788 ? It was this development (described by Mr. Inkerman Rogers) which led to the building boom of 1800-1814 during which Richard Chapman of Cleave-houses—whose mould-loft is still there—built sloops and bomb-ketches for the Navy. Anyway, business was brisk in 1788 and Bideford is at least the probable scene of Samuel's apprenticeship. There was nothing, admittedly, to prevent John Walters from sending his sons to Bideford while he himself remained at Ilfracombe. But Samuel's own account, to be quoted presently, reads as if he were living at home, while still a shipwright, in 1795. As he had served his time by then, his apprenticeship must have begun about seven years before. What of his education before that, up to the age of ten ? He was educated, he says, in " a school of Arts and Sciences "; a deliberately vague phrase, designed to make the best of what teaching he had had, presumably at Ilfracombe. What did it amount to ? Little enough, one would suppose. At the same time, it was obviously better than he would have received had he been living to-day. A shipwright then was very much more than a carpenter is now. He had eventually to design ships as well as build them. Thus Samuel, left ignorant of Latin and French, was able to write legibly and neatly, able to draw and tolerably proficient in mathematics. He had gained, too, a taste for literature. He had heard, he says, of Addison, Locke, Johnson, Swift, and Goldsmith. Some of this culture he owed, by his own account, to his father's friends, George Coats, Thomas Chapman, and Robert Holland, " connoisseurs of the Age." Research has failed to establish the identity of these beyond the fact that George Coats was a Trustee of the Ilfracombe Meeting in 1772. They were, in all likelihood, a group of intelligent nonconformist tradesmen, far more literate than their descendants will generally allow them to have been. John Walters, the copier of hymns and sermons, was at least as intelligent and must at least share the credit for his son's education. It is possible that Thomas Chapman, incidentally, may have been related to Richard Chapman, the Bideford shipbuilder.

In 1796 Samuel Walters went to sea. It was a fairly natural step for any spirited young Devonian in time of war, even for one who, as a shipwright's apprentice, would be exempt from impressment. It was the third year of the war and there were great deeds to be done. But Samuel's motives were not, by his own account, as simple as that. They are best described in his own verse:

GENERAL LINES AND STANZAS.

In the eighteenth century there was born
In the sixth month, and tenth day, in the morn,
In the seventy-eighth year, 'tis very clear
Sretlaw Leumas did he then appear.

And when he had come to light
'Twas gratifying to his maternal parent's sight,
The name above transposed to view
Will demonstrate the truth to you.

Though of an indigent birth was he
And of a common calling was designated he,
But something hovering in his mind
Should he go abroad his fortune would find.

To his tender Mother one day did say
Though I now work hard, and no time to play,
Something inclines me to think I may
Become a gentleman some future day.

The same was heard by a neighbour near,
Poor Molly White it would appear,
When his gentle Mother thus did chide the strain
" Samuel, my dear, pray do not be so vain."

But as his trust was in all powerful God's aid,
Whose unerring guide induced him, 'tis said,
To go to India he engaged, and went away,
Tho' his father disapproved, 'twas ere break of day.

But very soon after he was gone to sea,
Busy people urged his Father to be
Acrimonious and ill-natured to his Mother dear,
Although his departure cost his Mother many a tear.

It was prognosticated, they would be bound,
In lefs than six weeks Sretlaw would be drownd,
As he naturally sleepy used to be at night,
And thus going to sea would not be right.

As these verses can be fairly regarded as of more biographical interest than literary merit, the editor may be excused for breaking off at this point, with a promise to give the rest of the poem later on. The picture so far is of a boy running away to sea against his father's wishes and amid the neighbours' gloomy forebodings. But the reader should be warned against thinking the affair more romantic than it was. For one thing, Samuel had waited to do this until he had served his time as a shipwright. For another, he had planned what ship he was to join. His entering on board the *Ocean* in London River was not an accident but something arranged beforehand, discussed, and finally decided upon against his father's advice. All this is apparent from the fact that his first ship was commanded by Captain John Bowen. This is significant simply because the Bowen family came from Ilfracombe and were the most important people—barring possibly the squire, Sir Bouchier Wray—in Samuel Walters' world.

The Bowens were a remarkable family and, like the Walters, probably of Welsh descent but from Glamorganshire. There were five in all, James, John, Richard, George, and Thomas, the sons of a merchant-service captain. James, the eldest, was born in 1751, and served in merchantmen until appointed Master of the *Artois* in 1781-1782. Being Master of the flagship at the Battle of the First of June, he was afterwards promoted and was a Rear-Admiral when he died in 1835. It was his connection with the Transport Board of the Admiralty, begun in 1789 and confirmed when he became a Commissioner in 1806, which established, to some extent, the family fortunes. Thus John, the second son and Samuel Walters' first patron, quitted the merchant service to accept a post under the Transport Board— a post which he held from about 1804 until 1810 and which involved supervising a small establishment of storekeepers at Dudman's Yard, Deptford; which establishment followed all Civil Service tradition by growing imperceptibly from five in 1804 to seventeen in 1816. Richard, the third son, was the brilliant one, for whom great things were predicted. Born in 1761, he served under Jervis and was soon commissioned. But even he owed his first command to the Transport Board—the command of a division of transports on a voyage to New South Wales in 1790. Posted in 1794, he was killed under Nelson at Teneriffe in 1797. His younger brother, George, served under him and was promoted Commander and later, Captain. The fifth son died as a midshipman in 1796. By 1810 both of James Bowen's sons were post-captains, one of them dying in the East Indies in 1812. The Bowens were, in short, a seafaring family of some note.

In 1795 much of this had still, of course, to happen. James Bowen (see also note on page 134) was then a Commander and Richard already a Captain and talked of as a future First Lord of the Admiralty. " Captain Bowen " wrote Jervis to General O'Hara " who is a child of my own, is selected to command the small naval force at Gibraltar and you will find in him the most inexhaustible spirit of enterprise and seamanship that can be comprised in any human character." That the Bowens were the local heroes of Ilfracombe—where Richard's monument may still be seen in the church—is fairly obvious. Samuel Walters must have looked up to them with awe during his boyhood, when James Bowen was chasing smugglers in the Revenue Cutter *Wasp*. Awe would have changed to veneration from 1794, when James had become famous and Richard achieved post-rank—soon to be called " *Terpsichore* Bowen " after his capture of the *Mahonesa* in 1796. Occasional glimpses of the Bowens may have had much to do with his idea of becoming a gentleman—a feat which James Bowen had, after all, just accomplished on gaining his commission at the age of 43. Samuel's acquaintance with them must have been distant enough, but it sufficed to gain him an appointment as Carpenter's Mate in the ship *Ocean*. This really implied no great favour on anyone's part—qualified shipwrights were not as plentiful as all that in wartime. Nor was the opening a particularly brilliant one. John Bowen was the least distinguished of the brothers and the *Ocean* was nothing very dazzling in herself. She must not be confused with the other East Indiamen of the same name—the 1,200-ton *Ocean* of the same period or the later ship managed by Sir Robert Wigram. John Bowen's *Ocean* was an extra ship of 461 tons, and not a regular Indiaman at all. Managed by William Hurry, Esq., she was taken up for one voyage in 1796 and for another in 1798. Her carpenter was George Puller, and Samuel Walters joined him as his mate on 1st January, 1796. The *Ocean* was then being fitted and coppered in Dudman's Dock.

Samuel's first voyage began when the *Ocean* dropped down to Gravesend on 18th February and on 7th March discharged her pilot in the Downs. Proceeding to Cowes, she there embarked (30th March) part of the 28th Light Dragoons before sailing with a large convoy on 11th April. The whole was at first under the orders of Admiral Sir John Colpoys, but the West India ships parted company on the 19th and the East Indiamen went on to the Cape of Good Hope, escorted by seven sail of the line under Vice-Admiral Sir George Keith Elphinstone. This squadron had more to do than protect the Indiamen; it was primarily sent to deal with a Dutch Squadron at the Cape of Good Hope. This squadron, heavily outnumbered, duly capitulated in Simon's Bay on 17th August. The East Indiamen (*Essex, Asia, Lord Camden, Lord Macartney, General Goddard, William Pitt, Nottingham, Manship, Alfred,* and *Ocean,* with the extra ships *Lion, Prince Frederick,* and *Ocean*) now went on their way (10th September), the smaller *Ocean* being among those bound for Bengal. In view of the gloomy predictions made by the Walters' neighbours it is interesting to note that a Samuel Walters—a trooper in the 28th Light Dragoons—died on board the smaller *Ocean* on 14th May, within six weeks of the convoy's sailing. The other

15

and larger *Ocean*, moreover, was in fact lost on 1st February, 1797—the news of which disaster might easily have reached the Walters' family and led his mother to conclude the worst. Samuel's own ship was not far, as we shall see, from sharing the same fate.

The smaller *Ocean* sailed from Bengal, laden with sugar, in company with the *Alexander, Prince Frederick. Haman Shaw, Friendship, Echo*, and *Latona*, on 26th March, 1797. They were escorted by the frigate *Fox* and her prize, the *Modeste*. There was work for the carpenter's crew of the *Ocean* on 26th May when—resulting from a hard gale in which the convoy was scattered—the starboard quarter gallery was broken and a leak started near the stern post. The crew were at the pumps until the Cape was reached on 11th July but other ships were in worse case, for the extra ship *Exeter* came in on 3rd August with "people all dead in the Scurvey." At the Cape there collected sixteen Indiamen all told, half of them extra ships, which sailed for England on 26th August under the protection of the *Sceptre* [64], *Stately* [64], *Raisonable* [64], *Jupiter* [50], *Dordrecht* [64], and *Sphinx* [20]. This was Samuel Walters' first glimpse of the *Raisonable* in which he was afterwards to serve. She was, he says, the first man-of-war he ever went on board—so he presumably visited her on this occasion. The homeward voyage via St. Helena was quite sufficient to test Samuel's vocation for the sea, as the following extracts from the *Ocean's* log will serve to show:

5 November. *Prince Frederick* leaking. Several Carpenters from the Fleet sent on board.

23 November. Hard gale. Pumping.

25   Captain very unwell.

26   Scaff of the Stem found to be damaged. All bolts broke.

27   A fair wind. *Thank God.*

1 December. Wind flying all round the Compass.

13   Saw Portland.

14   Came too in the Downs—12 weeks pafsage from St. Helena. All well, *thank God.*

The *Ocean* was at Gravesend on the 18th and in Long Reach on the 19th. The *Madrafs* Hoy was alongside on the 21st and the discharging of cargo began between decks and finished at Deptford on the 19th January, 1798. As the carpenter's mate, Walters would be one of the last men to leave the ship. He actually quitted her on January 22nd, and no doubt made his way back to Bideford or Ilfracombe, perhaps to be welcomed as one believed lost. In his own words:

But in lefs time, than two years
He put an end to all their doubts and fears,
By returning home in health so gay
Those dismal stories to drive away.

It may be that he was interrupted before he had narrated his adventures more than twice. Warriors of more recent years have known what it is to be cut short by civilians eager to show them the bomb-crater in the next street but one. In this instance the Devonians had the story to tell of the French landing at Fishguard in February, 1797. True, the landing was not actually at Bideford—just as the bomb had usually missed (by a fraction) one's own home. But the French had been *seen* off Ilfracombe and would clearly have landed there—no doubt of it—had it not been for the resolute appearance of the North Devon Regiment of Volunteers under Colonel Orchard.

One may believe that Samuel had not forgotten to bring oriental gifts for his young sister, now aged ten. As for his elder brother, Miles, there is reason to believe that he too had gone to sea. No details of his early career seem to be known, but that he was a sailor, and also a carpenter's mate, seems very probable. Granted that to be so, his failure at sea, perhaps because of illness or accident, is almost certain. He is ashore, and not particularly prosperous, when we next hear of him.

What of Samuel's comparative success? About this two things are apparent; he had become a sailor and he was already studying navigation. The return voyage in the *Ocean* must have tested everybody on board and the carpenters not least. From this test he had emerged with credit as a seaman as well as tradesman. Apart from that, his bookish tendency had led him to study nautical astronomy, perhaps with the help of someone on board. Altogether, he had favourably impressed Captain John Bowen. This would have been more immediately useful had John Bowen been destined for a long career in the Company's service. Actually, he was to retire from the sea fairly soon, probably from illness, and secure (as we have seen) a Civil Service post under the Transport Board. This may well have been his last voyage, the final " thank God " in his log representing his intention, once safely ashore, to stay there. Be that as it may, he evidently recommended Samuel Walters to his brother, James Bowen, then taking command of the *Argo* [44] in the Downs; and James, it is equally evident, promised to keep an eye on him. This is his entry in the *Argo's* Muster Book:—

Bounty paid.	No.	Year.	Appear-ance.	Whence & whether Prest or not.	Place & County where Born.	Age at time of entry in this Ship.	Men's Names
5.0.0	750	1798	Mar 23	Vol'r	Ifracombe Devon	21	Sam'l Walters ab to 1 May 98 then Mid

It is clear from this that he was taken on the quarter-deck with a promise of midshipman's rank as soon as a vacancy should occur, as it presently did.

Samuel Walters was thus given his chance in life. His ambition to become a gentleman no longer seemed as wild as it had appeared to Molly White a few years before. As Able Seaman (not carpenter's mate) he was in line for promotion. He was in the Navy, which was less exclusive, in a way, than the East India Company's service. It was wartime with the Navy expanding and needing more officers every day. The *Argo* was bound for the Mediterranean where there was sure to be fighting. There would be prize-money, a commission, a single-ship action, mention in the gazette, the command of a sloop, post-rank, knighthood, perhaps, and then—anything was possible for a man with ability and luck. It might mean a hero's death, like Richard Bowen's. Or it might mean the steady rise which rewarded the solid ability of James Bowen himself, just deservedly posted and now equally in favour with St. Vincent and Howe. They were great days to be living in ! Day-dreams apart, young Walters was certainly entering as good a school of seamanship as he could have found. The middle-aged Captain Bowen, with his long experience as Master, was a model seaman and those about him— William Miller the First Lieutenant, Thomas Pitt the Master, John Ward the Boatswain—would be men who knew their trade. True, the *Argo*, a rather obsolescent two-decker built in 1781 and sister-ship to the *Roebuck* of 1774—was not a crack frigate of the 38-gun class. But she would do to begin with. There was even a schoolmaster on board (Mr. Sam'l Dixon) to teach navigation.

Apart from the likelihood of learning his trade, what solid grounds had Samuel Walters for any optimism he may have felt ? Putting luck on one side, promotion mostly depended on the recommendation of superiors; an " interest " in the service to be gained by birth, by relationship or by exceptional merit. Now, the Bowens were probably willing to forward young Walters' career up to a point; he was a Devonian, a neighbour and a likely lad. But their own interest was limited, their own origin fairly humble and Richard (their trump card) had fallen at Teneriffe. What was worse still, from Walters' point of view, was the fact that the Bowens were themselves so numerous. James Bowen had two brothers and two sons to think about before he could attend to anyone else. Both his sons, moreover, were to be on board the *Argo*—James, the elder, and John (aged 18), both midshipmen and both destined to achieve post-rank. Walters might deserve, and gain, Captain Bowen's protection in the service, but it was not for him that the Bowen interest would be strained to the uttermost. His turn would come, if at all, when all the Bowens themselves had been provided for. Thus, the younger James Bowen soon became Master's Mate, with an Acting Commission as Flag Lieutenant. This not being confirmed, he was a Master's Mate again in 1802. Perhaps as a result of similar efforts to promote John Bowen, Walters, who had become Master's Mate early in 1801, descended to midshipman again on 28th July in that year. Whatever his vicissitudes in rank—and they were the common experience— it is clear that it was in the *Argo* that he completed his knowledge of navigation, being fit, by June, 1800, to be entrusted with a recaptured Falmouth Packet. As he himself put it, in continuing the stanzas already quoted:

> In the Navy next he did appear
> Though his abilities was of an humble sphere,
> Self taught himself the art
> In navigation to do his part.

> To guide the Bark from shore to shore
> Was oft his task, thus he did explore
> Europe, Africa, and America to afsail
> And fortunate enough but once to fail.

What sort of a man was he? To some extent that will be shown by what he did, by what he wrote, and in what his portrait (see the frontispiece) can be thought to reveal. For the present purpose his own words are most apt, contained in the pages which he evidently intended as his preface and which are now printed as such. They were written, remember, long afterwards. They express not the lively expectations of his youth but the resignation of a faintly disappointed middle age. While thus false, in atmosphere, to his early life, this moralising tells us all he wished us to know of his youth. It betrays, at cross-purposes, the philosopher who has learnt to despise fame and fortune, and the autobiographer who is still sufficiently vain to conceal the exact nature of his original trade. It exemplifies his prose style at its best; and a very good best for one of his education. It shows how in later life he liked to picture himself. On one passage a comment may perhaps be forgiven. Where he speaks of his " fever of vanity", his " ravenous appetite after pleasure ", and his former " desire of notice from the great", we should remember some of the circumstances. His nonconformist origin should warn us against assuming that his desire for pleasure was ever more than very moderate by any standard but his own. His " desire of notice from the great", on the other hand, was probably real enough. He refers here, obviously, to the two months or so during which he was shipmates with Earl St. Vincent. It was an honour for which the small and obsolescent *Argo* was little prepared. The odds were a hundred to one against such a ship ever hoisting an Admiral's flag, however temporarily. To a young man like Samuel Walters the near presence of Earl St. Vincent—a man he might never have expected even to see—must have been overwhelming. It was also, in a sense, the chance of a lifetime. Supposing he could distinguish himself with the Admiral watching ? What if he could board an enemy ship, dirk in hand, before *either* of the young Bowens' boats had got alongside ? Or maybe rescue someone from drowning ? Lots of things might have happened to fix the name " Walters " on the Admiral's memory. "Ah", he would say (a few years later, when First Lord of the Admiralty) " that is the young man who dived from the fore-yardarm of the *Argo* in '99. He should be promoted." Needless to say, no such heaven-sent opportunity arose. It never does. Walters no doubt carried away the memory of dining at the great man's table on two or three occasions, presumably too petrified to utter a word. Apart from that, he probably made frantic efforts to be more efficient than any midshipman had ever been before—his deck in better order than seemed humanly possible, his topmen up the rigging almost before the order could be given. But all, evidently, was in vain. Perhaps the Admiral had something else to think about. Perhaps, indeed, he was not easy to impress.

PREFACE

By Samuel Walters.

W E never begin to think justly until time and circumstances render us in some measure independent of the commonly received opinions and prejudices of men; in short, not until we arrive at that happy climacteric [of] the understanding when the pleasures, the cares, and the profits of the world abate something of those fancied estimates and sink to their intrinsic value, happen when it may; when we care no longer for the opinions of Mr. Lee and Lock any farther than the opinions of Mr. Lee and Lock go along with truth; when we begin to be only commonly civil to folly, and cease to be obliging to vice in any station.

It's neither honors, nor wealth, nor age that are capable of producing so desirable a point of wisdom. Honors may create pride; wealth, self-will; and age may confirm prejudices. They are the friends of error and serve to fix us in absurdity. It is then philosophy only that can dispose us to think justly. The man who has suffered the fever of vanity, the ravenous appetite after pleasure, and the desire of notice from the great, may hail his convalescence from certain symptoms; an inclination to retire to his own room, to seat himself on his sofa near the fire, to shun the world not from ill-temper, but from the just view of the uncertainty and precariousness of the tenure by which its pleasures and vanities are held.

Let not my readers imagine, by these observations, that he is a rigid essayist, with a brown wig and green spectacles, mumbling anathemas against the bad manners of the age. In truth, it is not so; he is yet of middle age, fond of pleasure in a certain manner, not to amount to dissipation, and am one against whom his better judgment has scored up innumerable reckonings of follies and indiscretions. Yet have I ever loved virtue, admired prudence, and honor'd the good in every station.

But before my reader sets out on his travels through the following pages, it may be well for him to become better acquainted with the author. Allow me, on this occasion, to say a few words of himself and of the sentiments of his mind, lest any one may find it convenient to say " No, I will not go this road; I do not like my companion." Then he will tell you honestly and candidly that he is not a disciple of the new philosophy, yet he was educated in a school of Arts and Sciences; he began to entertain a respect for Literature early among the friends of his father, who were known to many, viz., George Coats, Thomas Chapman, Robert Holland, and many more excellent men, connoisseurs of the Age. Books were his delight, and his occupation was reading. He had heard of Addison, Locke, Johnson, Swift, and Goldsmith.

He, the author, was born in what is commonly called the Garden of England, opposite S. Wales, in the middle of the reign of George III (of blessed memory) and was in the truest meaning of the word a person of quiet study, loving books beyond every other amusement. A desire, however, to go to sea tempted him to forsake the natural alliance his mind had formed, but it appeared as if it was only to take him from books at home, in order to make him conversant with the world (the Book of Nature), and mankind in general. His first voyage (ship *Ocean*) Cape of Good Hope, India; Mediterranean (His Majesty's Ship *Argo*); down Coast Africa, Channel, North Sea; (H.M. Ship *Raisonable*) East Indies, Cape, River Plate, South America; (H.M. Ship *Courageux*) Sweden, Denmark, Russia, and Norway; displayed their treasures to the riper understanding. He had left his natal home.

But in every clime he had found Virtue and Humanity; in every country, Providence, and in all the space he traversed, a Deity. The same sun arose from the Horizon of India as had cherished the soil of his paternal land (Devon), and tho' another hemisphere presented other stars, and Bengal another country totally different in its scenery, its productions and its costume, yet everywhere he could trace the strong outlines of the same Almighty I AM.

PRINCIPAL OCCURENCES IN HIS MAJESTY'S SHIP *ARGO* [44]
COMMANDED BY THAT CLEVER FELLOW AND ZEALOUS GOOD
OFFICER JAMES BOWEN ESQR., AFTERWARDS COMMISSIONER,
TRANSPORT BOARD, AND OF THE NAVY, IN THE PEACE [OF] 1815.

Date	REMARKS, &c.
March, 1798.	Joined the above Ship in the Downs, who had the gun vefsels and Bombay ships under Commodore Bowen's orders till the beginning of May, when the *Argo* was ordered to join a Squadron cruising off Havre de Grace, under Sir R. Strachan in the *Diamond* [38], and several frigates.
May 4th.	Picked up Captain Sir Sidney Smith, who had made his escape from France in a French fishing boat with several attendants. Landed him the following day at Portsmouth.
September 26th.	*Argo*, in company with His Majesty's Ships *Pomone* [40], Senior Officer, and *Cormorant* [20], with the East India [and] Lisbon [convoys,] and the convoy for the Mediterranean. Fell in with the enemy's squadron, *L'Hoche* ship of the line and seven frigates full of troops for Ireland, and by stratagem forming a line with India ships and hoisting as it were a Rear-Admiral's flag on one of the largest, the weather being hazy had the desired effect and the enemy taking it for a squadron for the defence of the convoy stood from us. They however were most of them taken by Sir J. B. Warren.[1]
28th.	*Argo* captured a Spanish vefsel from the Havannah bound to Cadiz, laden with sugar, &c., the name of this vefsel *Nuostra Senora de Aldea.*
30th.	Anchor'd with the prize at Lisbon. Received Sir Charles Stewart, Genl and suite on board, and proceeded with convoy for the Mediterranean.
October 6th.	Left Lisbon. Overland dispatches arrived of the defeat of the French Fleet by Rear Admiral Sir Horatio Nelson off the Nile.

[1] See Note 1, page 134.

Anchor'd at Gibraltar with convoy; the *Argo* was here attached then to an expedition against Minorca under the command of Genl Stewart and Commodore Duckworth, 4,000 land forces, &c.

Arrived a Squadron of Lord Nelson's Fleet under the command of Sir James Saumarez Bt. accompanied by most of the French prizes captured in Aboukir Bay, 1st August.

The expedition sail'd from hence for Minorca, very long passage occasioned by light winds.

On this morning made the land and landed the troops in Addea Bay; the Spaniards made off for City Della, and the troops met but little opposition.

The *Peterel* [16] Sloop which had been dispatch'd previous to the expedition coming near the Island, in order to reconnoitre the enemy's coast, was captured by a squadron of Spanish frigates, which on the 12th were seen from the signal stations at Minorca, when the ships of war put to sea after, but in consequence of a long chase the Commodore was obliged to relinquish it and the only one taken was the *Peterel* by the *Argo*, tho' the *Centaur* was within chase shot of the rear frigate when they gave it over.

Minorca and its dependencies capitulated to the above officers, &c. From this period the Captains were chiefly employed settling the affairs of the Island and Prize Property.

The *Argo*, surveying the Island, did not complete it till beginning of December, when she arrived at Mahon Harbour.

I, S. Walters, Xmas day, being nearly drown'd by afsisting with the *Argo's* boats in saving the crew of Spanish brig, prize, on shore in the entrance of Port Mahon.

Cruising about the Island.

Captured after chase of 10 hours, *Santa Teresa*, 38-gun frigate in company with the *Proserpine* her consort full of troops from Carthagena for Majorca, where they was at anchor when discovered by *Argo* and *Leviathan*; the latter frigate [*Proserpine*] escaped.

Burnt in the River Tortosa (a branch of Ebro) nine Spanish merchants coasting vefsels, 40 to 50 tons, laden with Naval Stores, altho we had [taken?] one light vessel outside the Bay. Notwithstanding they were all aground close to the bar, not a mile from the entrance, burnt them at night, the enemy having collected force to prevent recapture. **Bad, Bad.** Lt. Findley.

March 20th. Captain Bowen sent on an embassy to treat with the Dey of Algiers to supply the Island of Minorca with livestock, &c., who was very graciously received, and a number of presents presented by the Dey to the Commodore and General and the Captain (Bowen), not the least of beautiful Arabian Horses, &c., &c.

April 18th. Return'd to Port Mahon with live bullocks, &c.

April 30th. Captain Bowen again sent to Algiers having transports under convoy of the *Argo* for livestock from Algiers. Went to Bona and there loaded transports [and] returned to Port Mahon.

May 29th. Found the Commodore and Squadron had put to sea to join Lord St. Vincent's Fleet, which came in the Mediterranean Sea in quest of the combined Fleets of the enemy, of France and Spain, which had, it appears, escaped from their ports, notwithstanding the vigilant watch on them.[1] *Argo* compleated water and wet provisions and put to sea as per orders left to do so, in quest of noble Earl's Fleet.

31st. Joined it this day in the Bay of Rosas.

June 1st. Anniversary of the memorable Lord Howe's Action in which our gallant Captain was Chief Pilot,[2] and whose boat was swamped alongside Rear Admiral Duckworth's ship the moment after Capt. Bowen was out of it, but [through] prompt assistance on board the *Leviathan* no lives were lost.

June 2nd. This day Vice Admiral Lord Keith joined the Fleet in the *Queen Charlotte*, with several ships of the line, and succeeded the Venerable Earl of St. Vincent in the command of this august Fleet, who proceeded in the *Ville de Paris* to Port Mahon where the *Argo* soon arrived.

23rd. Embark'd on this day Lord St. Vincent and suite, Captain G. Grey, Lieut's Maitland and Baird and others.[3] The same day sail'd from Port Mahon.

July 5th. Anchor'd at Gibraltar the evening of that day. Lieut. Maitland, reconnoitring the combined Fleet which were in

[1] See Note 2, page 134.   [2] See Note 3, page 134.

[3] Capt. Geo. Grey was 'Adjutant-General' or is so described in the *Argo's* Jog. The others included Mr. Benjamin Tucker, Secretary, Mr. W. Jackson, Master Attendant afloat, and Mr. P. S. Tracey, Secretary to Capt. Grey.

sight of the Rock, in the *Penelope* Cutter, [it] being calm, drifted among it and was captured by a Spanish frigate.

July 6th.

The Spanish ships of war forming the Van Division of this fugitive combined Fleet, passed the Rock. Light winds and calms preventing Lord Keith getting any knowledge of the

10th.

enemy. However, the easterly breeze came when the rear, composed principally of French, passed the Rock.

11th.
14th.

Following morn at daylight weighed and proceeded down the Straits to-day and watched the enemy. On the morn, being close in with Cadiz, saw the combined Fleet there at anchor, but at noon (wind N.W.) two ships of the line and a frigate gave chase to the *Argo* until near sunset working after us, the *Argo* keeping her wind on the starboard tack. At 6 p.m. bore up with all sail for the Straits, and passed the enemy ships almost within gun shot and anchor'd the

15th.

following morning [in] Rosas Bay, Gibraltar.

17th.
21st.

Proceeded with dispatches from Earl St. Vincent to Lord Keith, fell in with the Fleet, Captain went on board the Flag, *Queen Charlotte* [100].

23rd.

Argo is anchor'd at Gibraltar.

24th.

Proceeded to Tetuan Bay with convoy of victualling ships for the British Fleet. Following day anchor'd in Rosas Bay.

July 30th.

Lord Keith's Fleet proceeded down the gut with fine east wind.

31st.

The following day, the venerable Earl rehoisted his flag, and the *Argo* soon receiving his suite weighed and proceeded down the Strait for old England. At noon between Cape Trafalgar and Cape Spartel.

August 10th.

Captured the Spanish Ship Packet *Infant Amelia* from Cavvano bound to the Havannah, richly laden; a pretty vefsel pierced for 16 guns, 10 mounted.[1]

1799.
August, 16th.

The *Argo* arrived at Spithead, with prize *Infant Amelia*. Saluted the Flag of the still more venerable Admiral Sir Peter Parker Bt.[2] The *Royal William* returned it. The *Argo* put in quarantine. The noble Earl and his suite was permitted to

September.

land at Portsmouth. Here the *Argo* remained till the beginning of September when she was ordered to Sheernefs to be docked and repaired.

[1] The *Argo* had fifty Spanish prisoners on board for the homeward voyage, destined for Porchester. She must have been horribly crowded.

[2] Admiral Sir Peter Parker was then aged 78

September 16th.	She was put into dock, remained 17 days there.
October 3rd.	Warped out of dock, employed in repairing and fitting new
November 16th.	rigging, &c. At length, being complete in stores, &c., went
	out of harbour, anchor'd at the great Nore.
25th.	Sail'd from thence, passed through the Downs.
26th.	Anchor'd at Spithead. Lt. Malpass succeeded Lt. Pridham.
January, 1800.	Sail'd in company with His Majesty's Ship *Pomone* [40] and
	convoys for Lisbon, Mediterranean, &c. From continual
	blowing weather from west to W.N.W. obliged the *Argo* to
13th.	put into Torbay with the convoy. Here was Channel Fleet
	under Command of Sir Alan Gardner. Put to sea again.
20th.	N.E.-S.W. gale, anchor'd in Falmouth Harbour with convoy,
	following day arrived H.M. Ships *Boadicea* [38], *Anson* [44],
	and *Severn* [40].
28th.	W.N.W. put to sea again being moderate, in company with
	the Squadron and convoy. Next day a gale, bore up and again
	anchor'd in Carrack Roads. Squally boisterous wr.
February 13th.	This weather prevailing until this day when the *Pomone*,
	Argo, and *Cormorant* [20] with *Hindostan* [Storeship], and
	respective convoys put to sea. N.E.
26th.	Being already off Oporto the *Argo* parted company with her
	convoy for that port. It being blowing weather, easterly, the
	convoy could not attempt going over the Bar. There being a
	number of Spanish privateer cruisers on the coast, the *Argo*
	was obliged to be very vigilant in watch her convoy in order
	to prevent their being captured.
March 1st.	Captured after short chase the *Independant*, Spanish lugger
	privateer, 4 guns and 36 men. Sent her into Oporto.
	Following day captured *St. Anthony*, a lugger of the same
	description.
29th.	Carried away the fore topmast in chase of a Spanish schooner
	privateer, by which accident one man was killed, one drown'd
	and several had contusions, by which also the privateer
	escaped being taken. The next day, some time ere the top-
	mast was completely ready to set sail, a cutter cruiser was seen
	carrying all sail to reconnoitre the *Argo*. When she made us
	out she edged away free [and] set all her sails. We com-
	menced chase after, and by noon got within gun-shot of
	her when we commenced [firing our] bow chase guns. 50
	is supposed fired and not one shot struck her, and they having
	got the *Argo* (on the turn) on our masts she could not gain

the smallest on the chase. At setting of the sun, being near the Burlings, gave over the pursuit.

June 25th. This day recaptured the *Jane* brig, packet, which had been previously taken by the French cutter privateer *L'Vengeance* after a long chase. She was from Falmouth bound to the West Indies, her mail was sunk. In this vefsel I (Saml Walters, a midshipman) was sent on board her to take the charge and command of, with 10 seamen, with verbal orders to keep company with the *Argo*, but if separated by gales or otherwise, after a certain time to open seal'd orders, which took place the following day.

28th. S.W. A hard gale; bore up for Falmouth where we arrived safe.

Samuel Walters' memoirs do not cover the whole of his service in the *Argo*. Whereas he ends his narrative in June, 1800, his service in her did not conclude until April, 1802. The intervening period was at first spent in convoy work, notably in escorting East Indiamen to St. Helena on their outward passage. For his conscientious discharge of this duty Captain Bowen was afterwards thanked by the East India Company and presented with £400 in plate. He was promoted to command the *Dreadnought* [98] in 1803 and became shortly afterwards a Commissioner of the Transport Board. But Walters had quitted the *Argo* before that, being posted to the brig *Monkey* [14], probably to give him greater experience at sea at a time when (since the Peace of Amiens in October, 1801) many ships were being laid up. He evidently had only a few days leave before joining the brig. The *Monkey* cruised uneventfully in the North Sea and on the Dutch coast, being successively commanded by Henry Weir, James Tillard, and William Tatham. On her return to England in September, 1803, war having broken out again on the 16th May, Samuel Walters was transferred as Master's Mate to the *Ville de Paris* [112], flagship of Admiral the Hon. William Cornwallis, Commander-in-Chief in the Channel. Captain Bowen's influence can be discerned here, he having been Cornwallis's flag-captain, in the *Dreadnought*, until July 9th. Walters' promotion had obviously been decided upon and it was now a question of finding him a vacancy. On the 24th November, 1804, he was appointed Acting-Lieutenant in the *Goliath* [74], Captain Charles Brisbane. The squadron of the Channel Fleet to which the *Goliath* belonged—about ten ships—was at this time in Torbay, in an interval between spells of close blockade duty off Ushant, and actually put to sea that evening at 6 p.m. The occasion was marked by the wreck of the *Venerable* [74], Captain Hunter, which ran on a rock. The

Impetueux and *Goliath* were the nearest ships and sent their boats to pick up the survivors. These, with the *Frisk* cutter, saved the whole of the crew, Walters himself commanding the *Goliath's* boats. For some reason, perhaps through acting more promptly, Captain T. Byam Martin of the *Impetueux* was given all the credit for this rescue. After a further spell off Ushant, Cornwallis's ships were driven off by gales and returned to England for shelter, subsequently concentrating in Bantry Bay. Walters resumes his story at the point when he was confirmed by the Admiralty in his Lieutenant's rank, the news arriving on the day before he was posted to the *Raisonable* [64]—that is, on the 8th March, 1805. It was, it is obvious, a great moment in his career. He had realised a part, at least, of his boyhood's ambitions. He commemorates it not only in prose but in verse; the final portion of the " Lines and Stanzas," of which the remainder has already been printed:

> His good fortune was realised in the ship so famed
> On board of which Nelson first enroll'd his name.
> In the self-same ship Walters confirmed to be,
> Lieutenant was, and how he did fare you'll see.

PRINCIPAL OCCURENCES COMMENCING 9th MARCH, 1805, AND ENDING 31st AUGUST, 1810, [IN THE] AUSPICIOUS SHIP *RAISONABLE*, [64], BUILT AT CHATHAM 1768. BROKE UP AT [SHEERNESS ?] 1814.

Lieutenant Samuel Walters appointed to His Majesty's Ship, *Raisonable* [64] per commifsion bearing date the 9th day of March, 1805, being the day after my confirmation to the *Goliath*, having been acting in that ship per order of Honble William Cornwallis, Admiral of the White, &c., &c., Channel Fleet, since the 24th day of November 1804. The *Raisonable* was at Bearhaven in Ireland. The whole of the Squadron being in want of repair, consisting of five sail of the line, they were all ordered to the different Naval ports, the *Raisonable* ordered to Plymouth to be dock'd. Captain Barton being appointed to the *Goliath*, Capn. Josias Rowley[1] was appointed to succeed him in the command of the *Raisonable*. We arrived at Plymouth in the beginning of April, and was dock'd and fitted for foreign service. When she was compleat she went

[1] Josias Rowley (1765-1842) was of a naval family and had been a Post-Captain since 1795. He was to have a distinguished career, becoming a Baronet and a K.C.B. and living to be Commander-in-Chief in the Mediterranean in 1833-37.

out to Cawsand Bay. On the 19th May, Vice-Admiral Collingwood arrived from the eastward with eleven sail of the line. The *Raisonable* was also put under that Admiral's orders, and on the 22nd of May we saild for the Channel Fleet and joined on the 25th instant, consisting of 24 sail of the line under the command of the Right Honble Lord Gardner, which with our twelve made 36 sail. The whole Fleet stood close in to Brest and wore in succefsion, a very pretty sight. In the evening the *Loire* Frigate joined to leeward under a very heavy prefs of sail, with the signal out that she had been chased by an enemy's Squadron of five sail of the line, and as many frigates. It was supposed that those ships was the Rochfort Squadron which had escaped out of that port sometime ago on their return from the West Indies.

Admiral Collingwood on the following day was detached with ten sail of the line off Cadiz to reinforce the Squadron already there.

Soon after we were detach'd with a Squadron under the command of Rear Admiral Sir Thomas Graves, K.B., six sail of the line and a frigate, viz.

Squadron

Foudroyant [80].	Rear Admiral Graves
Barfleur [98]	Captain Martin
Windsor Castle [98] .	Capn. C. Boyle
Repulse [74]	Capn. Honble A. K. Legge
Triumph [74]	Capn. Inman
Warrior [74]	Capn. L. H. Linzey
Raisonable [64]	Capn. Jos. Rowley
Egyptienne [44]	Capn. Honble W. Fleming

When we arrived off Rochfort, reconnoitred and observed five line of Battle Ships, and several frigates in the roads. Blockaded this port. Calm, with fine weather and light winds. Anchor'd the Squadron until the arrival of Rear Admiral Stirling[1] in the *Glory* [98], to succeed the former Admiral in the Command, who frequently used to go thro' several Naval manœuvres, &c., &c. Nothing happened worth remarking.

On the 13th arrived from the Channel Fleet with Dispatches from Admiral Cornwallis, the *Atalanta* Sloop; these Dispatches

[1] Charles Stirling. Post-Captain in 1783, he had been with the Quiberon Expedition in 1795, at Algesiras in 1801, and (as Commissioner) at Jamaica 1803-4, achieving his flag in the latter year.

proved to direct Rear Admiral Stirling to reinforce Vice Admiral Sir R. Calder, then cruising off Cape Finisterre in quest of the Combin'd Fleet of France and Spain, expected from good intelligence to be on their return.[1] We joined Admiral Calder's Squadron of eight ships of the line and a frigate on the 18th, which made altogether a fleet of fifteen sail of the line and two frigates, a cutter, and lugger.

Remarks, &c.
May, 1805.
Channel Fleet ships,
viz.: –
1. *Foudroyant*. [80]
2. *Windsor Castle* [98]
3. *Barfleur* [98].
4. *Repulse* [74].
5. *Triumph* [74].
6. *Warrior* [74].
7. *Raisonable* [64].
8. *Egyptienne*. [44]

Vice Admiral Collingwood in the *Dreadnought*, with eleven sail of the line, was detach'd to go off Cadiz to reinforce Lord Nelson's Fleet on their return from the West Indies in quest of the combined fleet of France and Spain. On the following day we were also detached with a Squadron consisting of the ships named in the margin, under the command of Rear Admiral Sir Thomas Graves, K.B., to cruise off Rochfort. We had a very pleasant pafsage down, and on our arrival off that port we reconnoitred it, and observed there five sail of the line, one of which was a three-decker, besides frigates and brigs. We commenced a close blockade, occasionally anchor'd, and at other times performing several necefsary evolutions with the Squadron.

Very pleasant weather, nothing particular occured. Rear Admiral Stirling in the *Glory* arrived and succeeded Sir Thomas Graves in the command of the Squadron, who returnd to the Channel Fleet. Admiral Stirling, whenever the weather would permit, manœuvred the Squadron in every evolution that could be suggested. The French Squadron exercised sails and yards frequently.

June, 1805, *Glory* joined.

On the 13th instant joined the Squadron, from the Channel Fleet, the *Atalanta* Brig charged with dispatches from Admiral the Honble William Cornwallis. These dispatches, it appeard, directed Rear Admiral Stirling to reinforce another Squadron cruising off Cape Finisterre to intercept the combined fleet on their return from the West Indies.

13th joined *Atalanta*.

We joined Vice Admiral Calder in the *Prince of Wales*, with squadron of eight ships as per margin, making with our Squadron fifteen sail of the line, two frigates, a cutter, and a lugger. This superior Squadron was in high order and scarce a sick man in it.[2] Our cruising was from 42° to 45° North Latitude and from 10° to 12° of West Longitude.

July, 1805. 10th joined the Squadron under the command of Sir R. Calder.
Ships, viz.: –
 Prince of Wales [98].
 Hero [74].
 Ajax [74].
 Dragon [74].
 Malta [80].
 Defiance [74].
 Thunderer [74].
 Agamemnon [64].
 Sirius [36].
 Frisk [Cutter].
 Vile [Lugger].

[1] Under Villeneuve, from the West Indies.

[2] See Note 4, page 135.

Fine pleasant weather, and from good intelligence the combined fleet were expected to make Cape Finisterre. Ships of the Squadron were extended just as we could make out signal; one to the Southward, a second to the North'd, and a third to the Westward from daylight to sunset, when they came into line of battle.

About 11 o'clock the *Defiance*, one of the ships looking out in the S.W., made the signal that she had discovered a fleet. The necefsary preparations were made immediately for action. By noon we could count twenty-nine sail, of which twenty appeared to be of the line. The signal was made to make all sail and keep close order, and detachd ships to take their stations in the line.

22nd instant: Engaged the Combined Squadron.
English order of Battle:
1. *Hero* [74]
2. *Ajax* [74]
3. *Triumph* [74]
4. *Barfleur* [98]
5. *Agamemnon* [64]
6. *Windsor Castle*
   [98].
7. *Defiance* [74]
8. *Prince of Wales*
   [98].
9. *Repulse* [74]
10. *Raisonable* [64]
11. *Glory* [98]
12. *Warrior* [74]
13. *Thunderer* [74]
14. *Malta* [80]
15. *Dragon* [74]

The most prompt obedience was observed, every ship having as much sail as she could make. The *Dragon*, unfortunately, being to leeward, was not able to take her station, from her having the lookout when the enemy's fleet were first seen, thus we were likely to be deprived of her services.

The enemy's fleet appeared to be formed in a very good line and in close order; they had the weather gage of us, about two miles. Their frigates to windward, seven in number and two brigs, all of them close to the wind on the larboard tack; wind about N.N.W., fine pleasant weather, smooth water.

The Admiral made the signal to tack in succefsion and engage the enemy's centre when the van ship would fetch them, the *Hero* being the van ship. About 2.20 tackd and was followed by four others of the van, and before she had pafs'd the third ship of the enemy's rear it came on such a thick fog that it quite precluded our seeing the next ship ahead. About 3 o'clock the enemy's ships commenced action as our ships pafsed them on the larboard tack, but it was not returnd until the Honble Captain Gardner[1] of *Hero*, who led, had reached near the centre, when a most tremendous cannonade commenced and was kept up. This unfortunate fog proved to be very favourable to the enemy, as it disconcerted Admiral Calder's plan of attack; those near ships of the enemy engaged by our van on the larboard tack having tackd

[1] Alan Hyde Gardner, son and heir to Sir Alan Gardner, who did not receive a peerage until 1806. The son was not, therefore, an ' Honble ' at this time.

PLATE 1.—H.M. Ship *Argo* and H.M. Brig *Monkey*, shown off Beachy Head. Reproduced from a water-colour by Lieutenant Walters.

PLATE 2.—H.M. Ship *Ville de Paris*, near Spithead, flying the flag of Admiral the Hon. Sir William Cornwallis, Vice-Admiral of England, with Portland Bill on the right and the Channel Fleet in the distance. From a water-colour by Lieutenant Walters.

PLATE 3.—H.M. Ship *Raisonable* (on left) and H.M. Ship *Goliath*, shown together at Bearhaven, Ireland. Reproduced from a water-colour by Lieutenant Walters.

PLATE 4.—Shipwreck of H.M. Ship *Venerable* in Torbay, 24th November, 1804, her crew being rescued by boats from H.M. Ships *Impetueux* and *Goliath* and by the *Frisk* cutter. From a water-colour by Lieutenant Walters.

Remarks, &c.
July 22nd, 1805.
Noon.
Lat. 44° 0′ N.
Long. 12° 5′W.
Spanish Ships:
  1. America [64].
  2. Terrible [78].
  3. Ell Firma [78].*
  4. St. Rafael [80].*
  5. Espania [64].
  6. Argonaute [80].
The French:
  7. Indomtible [80].
  8. Swiftsure [74].
  9. Intrepid [74].
  10. Algesiras [74].
  11. Achille. [74].
  12. Aigle [74].
  13. Scipion [74].†
  14. Formidable [80].†
  15 Berwick [74].
  16. Atlas [74].
  17. Bucentaur [80].
  18. Montblanc [74].
  19. Neptvne [80].
  20. Plutо. [74].
F. Frigates:
  1. Hermione.
  2. Siene.
  3. Didon.
  4. Cornelia.
  5. Hortense.
  6. Rhine.
  7. Thames.
F. Briggs:
  Argus.
  Furet.
Those marked * taken
by Sir R. Calder,
† by Sir R. Strachan.
1805.
Most of the others
taken or destroyed by
Lord Nelson and
Collingwood.
October, 1805.

together, changed the position of the fleet; a thick fog coming on about the same time which precluded them from our sight and enabled the enemy to manœuvre greatly to their advantage in a fog. Their fleet was formed as they are described in the margin, the Spanish leading on the larboard tack when we first discovered them, and continued until this fog came on as before observed, when the rear of their fleet engaged by our van is supposed to have wore together, or as soon as they could ascertain the intention of the French Admiral who was in the *Bucentaur* in the rear of the fleet, fourth ship in that division. They must have come to the wind on the starboard tack and edged down into each other ships wake, by which the *Pluton*, former rear ship, became the van ship and leewardmost, for when it clear'd at intervals we found the whole line was on the starboard tack but very confused. The brunt of this action fell on the Spanish ships, for in the fog the Spaniards wore, bore up and came down and was sharply engaged by the British ships. The French ships made sail and got so far during the period of the engagement, that is, the major part of them which were roughly handled. The action commenced by the van 4.43; the whole of our fleet tacked in succefsion and engaged their opponents as they came abreast of them. At 6, abreast of the enemy, ships commenced firing and kept up a tremendous cannonade. The action about 7 became general, the *Windsor Castle* and *Barfleur* being well with the van ship were very much cut up, particularly the former, as some of the enemy's ships in the fog ran to leeward of them, and on hauling to the wind to close their van ships many of them were obliged to pafs them to leeward as well as to windward. At 6.40 observed a Spanish ship to strike; at 8 another Spanish ship of the line struck her colours; at 8.30 ceased firing, the enemy's ships too far ahead and to windward for shot to take effect. Ships in the van continued action. Some minutes after 9 o'clock the Admiral made the night signal to bring to on the starboard tack. Several shot hull'd the ship, and a great number pafsed through our sails and rigging, which were cut greatly. Our crofsjack and main top gall't yard carried away. Ten men kill'd and thirteen wounded, some severely. Employed getting up shot and wads, &c., expecting to renew the action at daylight. Ship's company remain'd at quarters all night. The ships that struck to our Squadron are those marked*, both seventy-four gun ships. They were taken pofsefsion of and soon after *St. Rafael's* masts went by the board, and the *Ell Firma's* main and mizen mast soon after. They were very much cut up, immense number of kill'd and wounded on board them.[1] The enemy's fleet to windward on the starboard tack. We remained at quarters all night expecting to renew the action at daylight. Light winds and pleasant weather, with a great swell. The enemy's fleet N.W. The Vice-Admiral made the signal general to know if any ship had occasion to lye by to repair damages; all answered in the negative except the *Windsor Castle* and *Barfleur*. The frigates were directed to take the prizes in tow per signal. Light airs inclinable to càlm. Observed the *Windsor Castle* to be very much cut up, fore-topmast, fore-cap, and top gone. The *Hero* was hull'd in several places between wind and water, as were most of the van ships of our Squadron. At 11 one of the enemy's frigates approach'd the Squadron to reconnoitre the state of it. The *Triumph's* signal was made to chase her, which made her make all sail back to his fleet. At Noon the van of the combined fleet N.W. by [West?] the rear, West; they were on the starboard tack and we on the larboard tack. At daylight Wednesday 24th, light winds and cloudy, the combined Squadron a long way off on the opposite tack. At 10-30 the *Defiance* made the signal that the enemy's fleet were going large, sixteen sail in sight from our mast head. The following morning the combined Squadron not in sight.[2] The whole of Sir Robert Calder's Squadron stood to the northward, prizes in tow, until the 2nd of August, when Rear Admiral Stirling's signal was made to resume his station off Rochfort with His Majesty's Ships *Glory*, *Triumph*, *Warrior*, and *Raisonable*, and *Nile* lugger. We went off that port and reconnoitred it and found the squadron that we left in port had sail'd; notwithstanding, the Admiral remained off that port in expectation of their return from their cruise. A few days after we were ordered to join the Channel Fleet. Variable winds prevailing, we did not join Admiral Cornwallis until the 13th instant, when the Captain went on board the *Ville de Paris* with his [despatch?].

[1] The *St. Rafael* had 167 casualties, the *Ell Firma*, 138.
[2] See Note 3, page 133.

34

The Admiral gave orders to be ready to close with the *Prince* by daylight in the morning to receive water and to complete provisions to three months. Our hopes of going into port was now at an end, we found that we were to be detached from this fleet on some secret expedition. By sunset we had received all the provision, &c., and the following morning we parted company with the Channel Fleet. Observed about the same time Vice-Admiral Sir Robert Calder joining with his fleet. We shaped our course for Cape Finisterre, all sail set. N.E. Fine breeze. At daylight the following morning, the 16th, we discovered a ship of the line to the Eastward, and three ships to the Westward. Suspicious of the one to the Eastward we exchanged numbers with [her], which proved to be His Majesty's Ship *Goliath*. By 8 o'clock she closed with us, and Captain Rowley went on board her to wait on Captain Barton, being Senior Officer, who informed our Capn that those three ships were the Squadron [which—together] with the *Fawn*, a corvette which the *Goliath* had captured the preceding day—made the 4 French ships which had captured the *Blanche* in the West Indies.[1] Moderate breezes and thick drizzly rain. The frigate and two corvettes standing towards us, *Goliath* and *Raisonable* laying to until it cleard. When they were not three miles off, they found out what we were; they bore up and made all pofsible sail. The wind freshened and we drew on them, our signal was made to follow the motions of the Senior Officer and carry all pofsible sail. About 2 o'clock the enemy's vefsels separated, the one hauld to the Southward, a second to the Northward, and the third to the Westward. The *Raisonable's* signal was made to haul to the wind after the Southernmost one, but this must have been a great oversight in the Senior Officer, as the *Goliath* was just out of port, full of provisions and water, while the *Raisonable* had but just as much water as would last her to Madeira, and of course must have been very light; notwithstanding we promptly obeyed the signal, but the moment we were close haul'd the chase left us, tho' Captain Barton did not discover it until near 4 o'clock, when he made our signal to chase the Northernmost one. Bore

---

[1] The *Blanche* [36], Capt. Zachary Mudge, was taken on 19th July by the French ships *Topaze* [40] *Departement-des-Landes* [22], *Torche* [18], and the brig corvette *Faune* [16].

up and made all pofsible sail, this appeard the largest, and we supposed it the *Topaze*, frigate. We appeard to gain on her a little, the *Goliath* coming up with her chase fast. About five o'clock her chase began to alter her course, and to bear up, soon after to make all sail, which the *Goliath* did also. Observed her to steer very bad, the *Goliath* coming up very fast. Thick drizzly rain, lost sight of them at intervals. At 7.40 observed the *Goliath* to open her fire of her chase guns, and the corvette return'd it smartly. At 8 it became very squally, observed the corvette to strike to the *Goliath*. This corvette proved to be *La Torche*.

The knowing Wm. Burch, Master H.M. Ship *Raisonable*; chasing and coming up with *La Topaze* which escaped from us and went into Lisbon.

N.B.—As bad a look out as could be, and all owing to the obstinacy of the Master, Cpn. following his advice.

Dark cloudy weather. Soon after lost sight of every vefsel. Kept in the same course. The darknefs of the night precluded our seeing them again til 11 o'clock. Observed a large ship pafsing on the opposite tack, supposed the frigate, tack'd immediately and made all pofsible sail in chase of her; kept pace with her at daylight. It freshened at 7, the frigate which was a very big one was nearly becalm'd, we kept the breeze. Observed the frigate to take in her water sail and set a ringtail, and run out stern chase guns. At 8.20 she hoisted French colours, and pendant. At 8.40 came alongside of her, but unfortunately for us it died away, calm, and the frigate carried off the remaining light breeze which favor'd us in coming up. Fired all the guns we could bring to bear on her; they appeared not to fire from more than six guns of a side. Their whole exertion with alacrity was made use of in trimming their sail, &c., &c. She went off with a top-gall't breeze, and we remain'd for upwards of an half hour totally calm. At last we got the breeze when she had gain'd from us upwards of ten miles. We made all pofsible sail, steering to the south'd; Cape Ortegal in sight. Continued in chase til the following morning when we lost sight of her.

23rd Arrived at Madeira.

Shaped our course for the Island of Madeira. After having a very fine pafsage made the Island of Porto Santo on the 22nd. Light wind, in consequence we did not reach Funchal Roads, Madeira til the following evening, when we came too near Loo Rock. Received good supplies [of] fresh beef and vegetables, which was a great treat, having been from May without tasting any. Overhaul'd and repair'd the ship and rigging, stopped several shot holes, got the ship in order again. Went up to Porto Santo. The English Consul with some of the principal

September.

Arrival of the Expedition against the Cape.

September, 1805.

Diadem [64].*
Raisonable [64].
Belliqueux [64].
Diomede [30].
Narsifsus [32].
Leda [38].
L'Espoir [Brig]
Encounter [Gun-brig].
Protector [Gun-brig].[1]

* Longitude West
33°00′
22°00′
fell 11°00′ too far to
the westward.

November.

Britannia [Indiaman].
King George [Transp.].

Arrival of the expedition at St. Salvador.

November, 1805.

The Expedition against the Cape of Good Hope from St. Salvador.

merchants accompanied us thither. Anchor'd in Porto Santo Bay. The following day the Chichester, store ship, with a convoy appear'd off, weighed and ran out and joined company. The next day anchor'd in Funchal Road. Anchor'd H.M. Sloop *Dart* and store ship with a convoy for the West Indies. In the evening arrived H.M. Ships *Chichester, Dolphin, Malabar.* On the 27th arrived the expedition from England, last from Ireland, under the command of General Sir David Baird and Sir Home Popham, supposed against the Dutch Colony of the Cape of Good Hope.

The Squadron [now] consisted of His Majesty's Ships [named in the margin] the East India Fleet consisting [of] fourteen sail, with thirty-nine sail of transports with troops, about five or six thousand Infantry, Cavalry, Artillery, and Company's troops. Watered and refresh'd the ships and troops. Being all ready on the evening of the 3rd October sail'd from Funchal Bay with the above ships in company with the West India convoy. The next day being a long way to the south'd and east'd the West India convoy parted company. Sir Home Popham hoisted a broad pendant and appointed the Captain of the *Diomede* to the *Diadem*, the Captain of *L'Espoir* to the *Diomede*, and the first Lieut. to be commander of the sloop. Fine pleasant weather; crofs'd the equator November the 3rd.* A few days prior to it, the *Leda*, with some of the fastest ships of the convoy were detach'd to go to St. Salvador to prepare and expedite getting water and refreshments for the expedition, but unfortunately going too near the Island of Ferdinandi Naronah where there are several dangerous shoals, in the night, the most part of the detach'd ships were in a very perilous state. The ships in the margin got on shore and were wreck'd; the troops and crews were saved except Brigadier General York of the Royal Artillery, and one private.

On the 12th inst. arrived at St. Salvador, commenced refitting. Ships watering, most of which was in want of it. This Harbour a very fine one, on the west side in the Bay of All Saints. Here we got for the refreshment of the expedition excellent supplies of fresh beef, fruit and vegetables, &c., &c. Everything on board, water complete and quite ready, left

[1] The *Protector* did not actually join the Squadron until after it had reached the Cape.

37

the Bay of All Saints the 29th instant. All in good health. Shaped our course for the Cape of Good Hope. We were employed in all the ships of War getting ready for landing, &c. The Commodore issued orders that each ship of the line should train (to small Arms, and pikes) two companies of seamen consisting of fifty each, to be commanded by a Lieutenant with two mates, or midshipmen, two quarter masters and a boatswain's mate. I was appointed to command the second of the two as Junior Lieutenant. The frigates to have one company each. The whole with the Marines were to be in a Brigade under the command of Captain Byng of the *Belliqueux*, to be attach'd to, and to land with the Army, to be employed as the Commander-in-Chief thought proper. The companies were numbered agreeable to the Seniority of the ships in sucefsion; to drefs with white jackets, blue cape and cuffs, white trowsers and gaiters. Each officer was directed to train his own company, so that it employed those who was appointed to command companies in fitting them out and drilling them twice a day. We had beautiful weather throughout. Sir David Baird visited the Ships frequently and inspected the different Regiments, and the best terms of friendly intercourse was on all occasions observed between the officers of the Army and Navy. We were very comfortable in this ship, having the Second-in-Command of the Army, Brigadier-General Beresford, on board; and Lieutenant-Colonel Gibbs, who commanded the 59th Regiment, on account of being very ill, removed to this ship from the *Pitt*, Indiaman. The Regiments that composed the expedition were as per margin. The command of the Artillery devolved on Major Spider. In addition to the number of troops in the margin there was a Regiment of Company's Recruits.[1]

24th ⎫
59th ⎪
71st ⎬ Regts.
72nd ⎪ Line.
83rd ⎪
93rd ⎭
20th Cavalry.
December.

January, 1806.

On the 3rd fine pleasant weather, made the land, a sketch of which is underneath.[2] At 4 in the evening the Table Mountain bearing E.S.E., the Commodore made the signal for the ships to cook three day's provision, and the Fleet to bring to for the night. Next day, light winds; stood in for

[1] That is, untrained European recruits destined for the East India Company's army in India.

[2] This illustration has not been reproduced.

Table Bay. At 5 p.m. the evening of the 4th, anchor'd with all the Fleet, Cape Town bearing S. by E., about half a mile N.E. from Robbin Island. The necefsary preparations was made for making a landing. The following morning 5th the signal was made at daylight to hoist out all the boats and put the troops in them, and to afsemble round the *L'Espoire* Sloop. Anchor'd close in to cover the landing. At 11 all the boats return'd and were hoisted in, being found impracticable to land from the great swell and high surf.

In the evening the *Diomede* [50] with the Transports, having on board Brigadier-General Beresford's Brigade, &c., was detached to land in Saldanah Bay.

The boats were again hoisted out at daylight and the troops put in them and the signal was made for the *Leda* to anchor in Lospards Bay, round which ship the boats were to afsemble. The *Encounter* and *Protector*, gun vefsels, were anchor'd between that ship and the shore. The enemy's Cavalry were approaching the beach in squadrons when the gun vefsels kept up a brisk fire which soon dispersed them. At 2 p.m. the boats put off and form'd abreast and effected the landing, the 71st Regiment in the van and received a sharp fire from the enemy's Rifle Men conceal'd in ambush, but was soon made to quit and a number of them were kill'd and wounded. Several of our's were wounded. The enemy now disappear'd and before sunset all the troops were on shore, Artillery, &c. &c.

This day promised succefs, and was only [spoilt by a] melancholy accident. A transport's boat with forty of the 93rd Regiment in, being too eager to [gain] the shore first— tho' one of the centre boats of the Division that landed— went the wrong side of the Channel, by which she upset and every soul in her went to the bottom and were drown'd.

In vicinity of Blueburg Mountains is several villages. It [was] reported that the whole of the Dutch Troops, Artillery, &c., had left Cape Town, castle and forts, and had taken up a strong and advantageous position about two miles to the Eastward of the foot of Blueburg Heights, [with] between four or five thousand men, Infantry, Artillery, Cavalry, Rifle Corps and Yaegers[1] [with] twenty-six pieces of Artillery cannon and a number of waggons. Lieut. General Janson, who was Governor of the Colony, commanded. They had also the crew

[1] Light infantry, skirmishers.

39

of *La Atalanta*, Frigate, about [two] hundred, who were attached
to the Artillery. Employed getting on shore water and
provisions, which by sunset were completely ready to advance.

At 2 a.m. we commenced our march towards the above
place. At 6 o'clock reach'd the Heights and came in view
of the enemy, which appear'd as reported to be in a very good
position, when we halted and took some refreshment being
near breakfast time. The Commander-in-Chief with the
principal officers was arranging the plan of attack. At 20
minutes past 7 the whole of our army drew up two-deep
from right to left, display'd the respective Colours of the
Regiments, and advanced towards the enemy. When they
conceived their Artillery would reach us they commenced
firing. Our Army,[1] from the run of the country being much
more level to the left, advanced rapidly. At 8 o'clock our
Artillery [being] in reach, unlimbered and opened our fire on
them. Soon after, the General finding the enemy's Artillery
was cutting up our left, orders was given to advance in column.
The 71st at the left of the line was in the van, followed by
the 93rd and 72nd, who advanced and [charged?] the enemy.
The 71st took two field pieces and several prisoners. At 20
minutes past 8 our Artillery ceased firing, the Enemy [having
retired?]

We did not reach the Army till noon with the Artillery
cannon owing to the extreme difficulty of the country to the
drawing Artillery. Seamen on this service drop'd down from
their drag ropes almost lifelefs—our water all expended—
and gain'd a little strength, and came running to join their
shipmates. Most of the enemy's cavalry kept on the Heights
during the action. The flank companies of the respective
Regiments were sent after them, and a smart action took
place in which Captain Foster of the 24th Regiment fell.
A brave soldier, pleasant companion, greatly respected and
universally regretted. Our kill'd and wounded about two
hundred; that of the enemy double the number. General
Janson retreated towards Hottentot Hollands Kloof, a place
if stock'd with provisions and water would be impofsible to
drive the enemy out of it, being by nature impregnable,
having only one chasm to enter, and that being fortified very

[1] Presumably he means the left of the two Brigades into which the infantry
were divided.

strong. Our Army at this time was situated between General Janson's Army and Cape Town, [he] being quite cut off from the latter. We halted for the night. At daylight the Army set forward for Cape Town, and at 3 p.m. halted near the lines. A Flag of Truce was sent out from the town to offer terms and treat for a capitulation, and was acceded to the following day, by which the Dutch were to give up to us Cape Town, Citadel, Forts, and lines, all the ships in Table Bay, all public buildings and stores, &c., &c., all Naval and Military men to be sent to Holland at the expense of the British Government, all French in the Colony to quit it.

The evening of this day, march'd on to Cape Town, took pofsefsion of it, halted in the parade square, a Royal salute was fired by our Artillery, and returned by Commodore Popham's Ship, the *Diadem*, the Squadron having all anchor'd in the Bay. General Beresford arrived just as we were marching in, with his Brigade from Table Bay. The Dutch Colours was haul'd down and the English Union hoisted in their stead. The Cape of Good Hope once more an English Colony.

General Beresford was [sent] with a force to Hottentot Hollands Kloff, and a capitulation [was arranged and] signed by which General Janson [surrendered upon terms, his troops to be conveyed to Holland?] accordingly at the expense of our Government. The Dutch troops march'd out, and the English took pofsefsion of arms, ammunition and artillery, twenty-six pieces, and a number of waggons and horses, the 18th day of January.

When the time was up that was allowed the General and troops to remain in the Colony, transports being prepared, the General and his family was put on board the *Bellona*, the finest and most accommodating ship; the troops on board of others. On their pafsing the *Diadem*, the Commodore's ship saluted the General, which was returned by the cartel's[1] manning their rigging and giving twice three cheers. It was suggested by Sir Home Popham and the General that we, with a small force, might succeed in making a landing in the River Plate.[2] It was soon determin'd on, and the ships in the

---

[1] A cartel was a ship employed in repatriating prisoners of war, especially those exchanged.

[2] See Note 6, page 135.

Diadem [64].
Raisonable [64].
Diomede [50].
Leda [38].
Narcifsus [32].
Encounter [Gun-brig].
    Transports:
Walker.
Willington.
Melantha.
Triton.
Ocean.

May.

Expedition against
  Buenos Ayres.

May.

June.

margin formed the Squadron. The 71st Regiment, a company of Artillery and a squadron of Dragoons form'd our Military force. The *Leda* being sent on to reconnoitre mifsed the squadron and did not join til the object of our pursuit was gain'd. The command of this little expedition was given to General Beresford. Being all ready we left Table Bay the 14th a.m. with a fine S.E. breeze. A few days after, the *Ocean* Transport having parted company, [we] shaped our course for St. Helena, where we arrived on the 29th inst.; the General and Commodore judging the *Ocean* would not join in time, solicited the Governor to allow some few of his troops to join, which he acceded to, and sent two hundred soldiers, some of whom were Artillery. This was a grand re-inforcement, and I think myself a plan'd thing that the *Ocean* should part company for a plea. Completed our water and left it the evening of 2nd May. The *Justina*, a merchant ship going to the Cape joined company for the river with us, being loaded with sundries for speculation. Fine pleasant weather. Commodore Popham ifsued a similar order to that of our going to the Cape, our force being rather small. Feathers and cloth was purchased at St. Helena for the purpose of drefsing the seamen train'd to arms for the purpose of co-operation with the Army, to be drefs'd with blue jacket, red cape and cuffs, white trowsers and gaiters, black caps and feathers. To consist of fifty men each under the command of a Lieut., two midshipmen, &c. Each ship of the line to have two companies; Frigates, one. To command the whole Marine Brigade Captain King of His Majesty's Ship *Diadem*; when landed to be under the command of General Beresford. On the 20th made the Island of Trinidad. In addition to the above seamen being train'd to be landed with the Army, the Marines was made up in the ships of the line to one hundred strong. On the 28th the Commodore shifted his broad pendant to the *Narcifsus* [32], and General Beresford came on board this ship. Sir Home went on ahead to make his observations, leaving the command of the Squadron to Captain Rowley of this ship. On the 8th June made the Isle of Palmer near Cape St. Mary's. From this a thick fog continued, only clear at intervals. About the 10th enter'd the River Plate, but on account of the fog did not see the *Narcifsus* til the 13th. The 13th it cleared. On the 16th the troops on board the ships of war were put on board the transports drawing the least draft of water. The General and Staff went on board the Commodore's ship, then the *Narcifsus*. The Marines and Seamen were put on board her also, and they proceeded for Buenos Ayres. Parted company the *Raisonable* and *Diomede* and took their station off Monte Video and Maldonado, occasionally anchoring to cut off all communication between those places and Buenos Ayres. Experienced some very heavy gales, principally from the N.E. Detain'd several Portuguese Vefsels. On the 7th July we had a violent gale from N.E. and shifted to S.W., commonly call'd a Pampyra by the Spaniards, in which we parted our best bower cable, near the whole cable [severed?]. Let go the small bower and brought up.

Diadem and *Raisonable* off Monte Video. *Diomede* off Maldonado.

July.

On the 9th came down from Buenos Ayres the *Willington*, transport with a supply of water, vegetables, &c., with the following account of the progrefs of our friends. They did not effect their landing til the 26th June, from having continual foggs with heavy rains, together with the *Narcifsus* having got aground on the upper part of Oyster Bank, greatly retarded their progrefs. On the 29th they had an Action with the Spaniards. Tho' four times the number of ours, they soon gave way in all directions, and the English advanced towards the City of Buenos Ayres. When General Beresford arrived before that City with his little force, a Flag of Truce was sent into the Citadel to summons it to surrender at discretion. When the Spanish troops march'd out and those of the English march'd in and took pofsefsion of the City, Citadel, Forts, &c., treasure to a great amount was found.[1] The General from good information was made acquainted that, the same day that he landed the English Force at de Barcagan, the Viceroy went off with immense treasure, ten or twelve waggon loads. Major General B., immediately he had got things a little arranged, detach'd a force in quest of them, and was fortunate enough to come up with and take a part of it. It was determined that the dollars should be immediately embarked on board His Majesty's Ship *Narcifsus* [32], and for her to proceed for England. I must now return to the *Raisonable*, on whose return after being obliged to put to sea join'd company the same evening the *Narcifsus* did off

Narcifsus and *Encounter* up with the Army at Buenos Ayres. They effected their landing near Ensenarda De Carrigan without lofs or opposition.

July.
Intelligence by the *Willington* continued.

Buenos Ayres Capitulation, 28th June.

---

[1] It amounted to 1,086,208 dollars, including that subsequently taken.

43

Monte Video from Buenos Ayres. A strong gale from the West'd parted the cable, small bower and was obliged to put to sea; haul'd to the South, this wind prevailing we drifted a long way to the East'd and blowing very hard most of the time, in consequence we could not reach our anchorage off Monte Video before.

When we joined the Squadron again this evening the *Narcifsus* came down having the treasure in, taken at Buenos Ayres. Sir Home shifted the broad pendant from that ship to his own, the *Diadem,* and the *Narcifsus* sail'd for England. The *Leda* join'd the Squadron, when the Commodore hoisted his pendant on board that ship and proceeded for Buenos Ayres, and we having lost two anchors and cables sail'd (to replace them and get other stores for ourselves and the Squadron, being much in want of sundry articles) for Rio Janeiro. We had very good weather until the

night. Dark, cloudy weather with thunder and lightning and heavy squalls and rain, wind E.N.E. At midnight one of those tremendous squalls split the fore and main topsail, jib, and foresail, unbent the remains and bent others. On the morning

running for Cape Frio thick foggy weather with small rain; at 6 it cleared, being just daylight when we discovered ourselves not above a mile and half from the shore of a fine sandy beach running off from very high land from E.N.E. to W.S.W. It proved to be the bay between Cape Frio and the south point forming the entrance of Rio Janeiro. Wore immediately and came to the wind on the larboard tack. It dying away, little wind, our situation became serious as the swell got up and we near'd the shore. At 6 a breeze drawing off shore. Frequent calms and light variable winds prevailing we did not anchor in the entrance of the harbour until the evening of the 14th inst.

In the morning sent an officer to wait on the Viceroy and report the arrival of the ship, which is customary to do so at this place. The pilot came on board to conduct us up to the anchorage abreast of the town of St. Sebastian, where we

anchor'd at one o'clock p.m. The Fort saluted us with 17 guns and we return'd 15, two lefs. Unbent sails and stripped ship preparative to caulking and refitting ship. The next day came off from the Arsenal a number of artificers and commenced caulking; careen'd ship to stop two shot holes received between wind and water the 22nd July, 1805, not having had an opportunity to have stop'd it before complete, it only was patch'd at Madeira. Received a quantity of boatswain's, carpenter's, and gunner's stores purchased for the use of the Squadron. Being all complete in the rigging, the ship caulked all over, &c., bent sails and prepared for sea. On the 4th drop'd down near Santa Cruz, the fare way, anchoring for leaving this place. On the morning the pilot came to take the ship out of the River, weighed and made sail with a fair wind out, N.N.W. Shaped our course for the River Plate. Fine pleasant breeze, promised a quick pafsage til the night of 12th, a strong gale with thunder and lightning and violent squalls with heavy rain. At midnight the main topsail was split, a piece out of the centre; most vivid lightning, not an interval of ten seconds between each clap of thunder; running about 9 knots per hour. A dismal night as I ever saw before or since; not an interval of a second without lightning, the most vivid; about 3 a.m. the fore top-gallant mast and fore-topmast was struck, and broke in three pieces each mast. It carried away the topmast, the foremast fractured about three feet above the cap, and the wreck came down. The lightning went clear of the cap, top and foremast head, it then struck the foremast about half-way up between the fore top and fore-castle deck, and took off all the outside part of the mast, the longest strip about twenty feet, and started several of the hoops, but on the carpenters' surveying it, the centre piece[1] of the foremast was found to be secure. Hove to and cleared the wreck; the carpenters employed preparing fishes.[2] A heavy swell with constant rain for three days, which greatly retarded the progrefs of the carpenters. On the 14th got the foremast hoop'd and woold'd. On the 15th fidded the top mast and swayed up the fore yard, crofsed the fore topsail yard. Shaped our course for the River Plate, being nearly abreast of the Isle of Palmer. Fidded the fore top-gallant mast and crofsed the yard. Made all pofsible sail, set stud'g sails; standing in to the River Plate. At sunset anchored between Maldonado and Iles de Flores in 9 fathoms water.

September 2nd

6th

September, 1806.
12th continued.

Struck by lightning.

Arrived 16th in the River Plate from Rio Janeiro.

[1] Evidently a 'made' mast, built round a core, not made from a single tree trunk.

[2] i.e., splints to strengthen the damaged part of the mast.

LINES ON HIS MAJESTY'S SHIP RAISONABLE, HAVING BEEN
STRUCK BY LIGHTNING ON HER PASSAGE FROM RIO JANEIRO
TO THE RIVER PLATE ON THE NIGHT OF 12TH SEPTEMBER,
1806, CITED IN A LETTER TO HIS PARENTS.   SEPT. 12TH.

This letter wrote in simple truth
At the very time in the prime of youth,
Announces treats of genuine love
But certainly inspired by God above.

1806.
At Rio de Janeiro.

This gallant ship quite replete
With various stores for the British Fleet,
On September of the very sixth year
To go to sea they did prepare.

By frequent thunder, storms so loud,
With vivid lightning in the clouds,
Though awfully grand in the dead of night,
Then struck the masts in pieces quite.

A gale of wind and seas so heavy,
Dark as pitch and no remedy
Except by Providence's aid and skill
Preserved us all from every ill.

This task perplexing, day dawn'd to see
The ungovernable Bark drifting fast on lee,
The land descryed on the lee bow
Then to wear the ship—could we tell how.

To any men but British Tars,
Might puzzle much, and increase fears;
Temporary sails in the prow being placed,
The bowlines gone, round in weather after braces.

And long she roll'd till on the other tack
The wreck being clear, a glafs of rum got Jack,
Willing and ready they all set to,
To get new topmasts up, this gallant crew.

When the evening of the second noon
All sail was set in the afternoon,
And bore away for the River Plate
For our Brother Cruisers to relate.

But on arrival at Fleet's anchorage, there
A very sad story we next did hear,
That Buenos Ayres had been retaken
And our little Army very much shaken.

But a small re-enforcement from the Cape
Induced the Commodore to try a feat,
To reduce Monte Video 'twas his intent,
But which proved abortive in the event.

                                    S. *Walters.*

In the evening anchored near His Majesty's Ship *Diomede* abreast of Monte Video. The Captain came on board and gave us the following account of the proceedings of the Army at Buenos Ayres—retaken by the Spaniards on the 12th day of August after having held out an unequal contest for several days, besides several skirmishes, in which our little force made a grand display of superior skill and judgement; only—short of numbers to cope with them—they at length were obliged to withdraw our men from the different outposts, and the whole of the English being quite exhausted, the General retreated towards the citadel, when every window became an embrasure and commenced firing on them in succefsion. At length they reach'd the citadel, when a church situated near the Citadel, where the Spaniards had a gun conceal'd, which also opened on them, our little Force [was] completely surrounded and overpowered. On the 12th August when General **Beresford** capitulated, the English march'd out with their arms and grounded them, and surrendered themselves prisoners of War.[1] Ships off this port as per margin.

Arrived His Majesty's Ship *Medusa* from the Cape, and brought us intelligence that a reinforcement was on its passage from the Cape, in *Lancaster, Howe, Protector,* and *Rolla* with four transports, 47th and 38th Infantry, 20th Cavalry. Employed distributing the Warrant Officers' stores.

Statement of General Beresford's whole Force.
Himself and Staff and officers and seamen R.N.
71st Regiment
Honble East India Co's troops, Marines, Dragoons.
Total 1,655.

September, 1806.

Monte Video, viz:
Diadem [64].
Diomede [50].
Leda [38].

17th

[1] See Note 7, page 138.

[On the] 29th arrived the *Howe*, the 21st Cavalry on board. Received from the *Howe* the troops on board her. On the 3rd October came out from Monte Video a Spanish vefsel from which vefsel we received several English prisoners under a flag of truce.

Arrived, viz.: 13th,
Lancaster [64].
Medusa [32].
Howe [Sloop].
Protector [Gun-brig].
Rolla.

Arrived the *Lancaster* and convoy with troops. It was determined on to arm four of the largest transports with four eighteen-pounders from the line-of-battle ships, and to fit a fifth transport as a bomb [vessel]. Small vefsels were kept off Monte Video to reconnoitre and watch the movements of the enemy. To complete this undertaking the Squadron and transports all anchored near the Isles de Flores, about three leagues from the main, so that it was impofsible for the Spaniards to make out or observe what we were about.

The *Lancaster* and *Diomede* was ordered to be lightened to $16\frac{1}{2}$ feet, and the plan of attack was to be as follows: The two ships of the line were to take their station close in with the North Gate, and to scour the batteries as they pafs'd them in succefsion. This battering squadron being complete

by the 28th. During the preparation of our battering ships the Spaniards form'd a large camp to the eastward of the citadel, and the tents increased every day. The peninsula on which the town is built, from the citadel, which is very well fortified, as well as the flanking batteries of the north and south gates, and the walls uncommonly high and strong, with a ditch all round it, consequently there could be no other method but battering it, or a regular siege by land, which our Military force was judged inadequate to. The Commodore and Captains, with the Colonels Backhouse (senior) and Vafsal, with the principal officers of the staff and other officers, determined, if possible, to effect silencing the

Ships and Vefsels
which form'd the
attack in line.
Van.
Triton
Hero
Royal Charlotte
Columbine
Fanny
Encounter
Protector
Leda [38]
Medusa [32]
Diomede [50]
Lancaster [64]

batteries with those ships prepared so that the Army should be landed under cover of their guns. It was considered another transport was wanted and immediately one was prepared as a bomb ship, which made the line as per margin, viz., the first three ships* besides being arm'd with ten to twelve twenty-four pound carronades had four long eighteen-pounders from the *Diadem*, and this ship, Captain Edmonds, who had first been superceded in the command of the *Diomede* by her former Captain, and who very handsomely volunteer'd to lead the line in, and was accepted by the Commodore when

48

PLATE 5.—H.M. Ship *Raisonable*. Reproduced from a water-colour
by Lieutenant Walters.

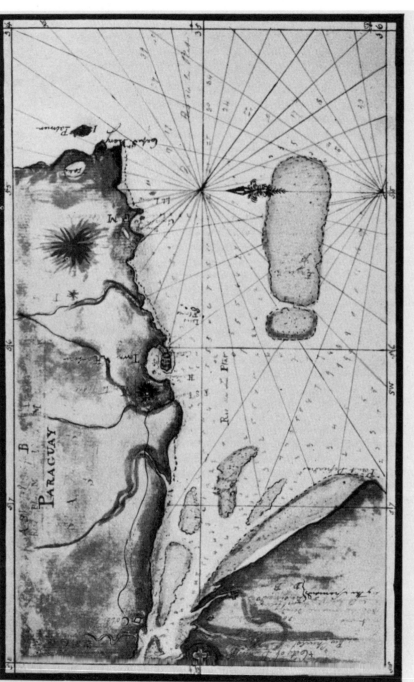

PLATE 6.—Chart of the River Plate, showing Buenos Ayres (extreme left) with Colonia opposite, Monte Video (centre) and Maldonado (right, near Cape St. Mary). From a sketch drawn and coloured by Lieutenant Walters.

he took command of the *Triton*. The next two vefsels† were bombs; all the transports under the command of the respective Lieutenants, Agents for them. A division of seamen were sent to each of them for working their guns, with mates, and midshipmen, and one hundred seamen sent from this ship to afsist the *Lancaster*, and as many from the *Diadem* to afsist the *Diomede*, in case of leaks from receiving shot between wind and water,[1] under the orders of a Lieut. from each ship. On the morning of the 28th October, all the fleet got under weigh and proceeded off the town, the troops on board *Diadem* and *Raisonable*. Fine pleasant wr. Wind about E.S.E. At 10, being well in, the signal was made for the battering ships and vefsels to attack the North Gate; Captain Edmonds in the *Triton* when he was in three fathoms made the signal, the guns did but just reach the shore, but as she ran along to the westward annoyed the batteries much. The Spanish gunboats kept up a quick fire as the arm'd ships [were] approaching the entrance of the Harbour. At 10.40 a smart fire was kept up on all sides, but it was found soon after, from the shoalnefs of the water it was impofsible to get the large ships close enough in to effect the object in view. The *Leda* telegraph'd her main deck guns only reach'd the shore when she was touching. The signal was made to discontinue the action, and close with the ships in the offing. From the above trial it was judged impracticable to succeed in getting the large ships close enough. In the evening the Squadron and convoy anchor'd abreast of Monte Video. By this time a number of ships had arrived from America and Europe, all of which were detain'd, or at least not allowed ingrefs to the ports of the River Plate, consequently they became under our care to look out for them. At midnight the *Raisonable*, for deception, hoisted a broad pendant and, the Commodore having ordered the troops on board the frigates from the ships of the line, proceeded with them and the gun vefsels for the Bay of Maldonado in the entrance. The following day the *Raisonable*, *Lancaster*, and *Diomede* with the arm'd ships, &c., weighed and made sail and ran down for the Isles de Flores. At noon anchor'd near them, received the men lent to the *Lancaster* and the arm'd ships. On the evening of the 30th inst. weighed in company with the *Howe* and arm'd ships,

Sir H. Popham's attempt to batter Monte Video and to land.

30th.

---

[1] Which was not unlikely in ships lightened as these had been.

and ran for Maldonado, and at 8 o'clock anchor'd in that Bay, and found the town in pofsefsion of Brigadier Backhouse, Colonel-in-Chief of the Army. The evening of the same day the Island of Govita was given up to the British on being summon'd to surrender at discretion to the Commodore and Squadron, and it was taken pofsefsion of the same evening, and the prisoners put on board the ships of war. The following is the narrative of the capture of the town of Maldonado: On the English Army being landed to the S.E. of it, they immediately proceeded for the town. Colonel Backhouse heard from good information that the greatest part of the troops who were in the town had gone off with most of the inhabitants into the country. A truce was immediately dispatch'd to summons them to surrender to the British troops. No answer being sent, our troops marched on.

The report the Commanding Officer received proved to be false, for the only people gone was the inhabitants that had left the town; and the troops (certainly most of them were rabble) had got on the house tops, lying flat down until our fellows were right under them in their march into the streets. At the entrance into this town there is a wood of prickly pear trees, their leaves being very large and so intermixed with each other that it was impofsible to discover if any men were the other side or not. However it proved that the troops who were reported to have gone into the country were in ambush, precluded by the above trees, and on the approach of the English, the Spaniards commenced bush firing. Our brave fellows, exasperated at their unfair proceedings, push'd on and put all they came up with to the bayonet. Numbers of ours were kill'd and others wounded. But when our fellows came past this thicket and made them out, and charged them, numbers of whom got off, they were then about a quarter of a mile from the town. Those which escaped the late skirmish retreated to St. Carlos, a small town distance about six or seven miles from this town. As was before observed, the house tops being covered with arm'd men, immediately our fellows entered the town, they commenced on them, by which great numbers of our troops fell.

Orders was given to break open and enter every house. By this great numbers were kill'd, tho' on getting up on the house tops (being all built flat with a hatch to go out on it),

November, 1806.
The Squadron in
Maldonado Bay.
Latitude 34° 40s.
Longitude 55° 10w.
Diadem. [64]
Diomede. [50]
Lancaster. [64]
Medusa. [32]
Leda. [38]
Howe.
Encounter.
Protector.
Rolla.

Force at Maldonado.
Infantry:
   38th, 47th.
   last three comp 54th.
Dragoons:
   Three troops 20th.
   Three troops 21st.

numbers of our fellows fell. In about one hour's time this dreadful seen of blood began to subside; silence succeeded the tremendous noise of musketry, and nothing was heard but the groans of the dying and the moans of those survivors for the lofs of their near and dear relatives, which so much embitters life. Our soldiers being very much fatigued, guards were planted, and the rest retired to rest. A number of prisoners were taken. It's a poor town, principally farmers and fishermen. To the south'd of the town is built a very high tower intended for a signal station. The intention in taking Maldonado was that our Force being too small to land against Monte Video, and the Commodore and the Colonels being of opinion that reinforcement shortly would arrive, induced them to take this place for the purpose of getting fresh beef, &c., for the troops and crews, of which we stood greatly in want of. This country being so well stock'd with oxen (upwards of five hundred in herds) and this place being situated about a half a mile from the place where the boats land, from the town, we had only to send on shore a few men arm'd with muskets and drive as many as was wanted for present use down towards the place where we used to kill them and take off the beef. Here the inhabitants, I mean the original South Americans, a strong laborious set of people, would attend for a very small pay, and well worth seeing; they throw a lacy [lasso] with such dexterity and precision, that they are certain of entangling the poor bullock, which after the man has thrown the bolo he gives the animal as much of the line as allows him to make off from twenty to thirty yards, when the running off has occasioned the lacy to get round three out of the four legs, by giving it check on a sudden ! Down comes the poor beast, and it is their fashion to hamstring them at the moment it falls, and pith him immediately, so that the ox suffers nothing in comparison to that of knocking it down and cutting the throat. By this we got a bountiful supply without either risk or much trouble. From the town to the east point which forms the bay of Maldonado and Govita Island, having three batteries on it within half gun shot of the main, a flat low sandy point for upwards of three miles, and for a mile at the extreme point in, and about a mile and half wide, was a beautiful green plateau of good grafs, where we might keep from two to three hundred head of cattle. To protect it, the *Raisonable* was anchor'd within a cable's length of the shore. The whole of the peninsula was under cover of her guns. It was also a safe place for our Army to retreat to in case of their being overpowered by the enemy, or deceived by any false information. We found it remarkably pleasant. Fishing, shooting, hunting, and riding was the order of the day, or visiting the Army at Maldonado. The frigates and small vefsels watching the movements of the enemy off Monte Video, that place [was] declared to be blockaded by the British Squadron. The three American merchant vefsels coming out were detain'd by the Squadron, the two former ones sent to the Cape, the latter Sir Home Popham and retinue went to England in, not being allowed a vefsel of war.[1]

Truth.
Bounty.
Rolla.

[1] See Note 8, page 139.

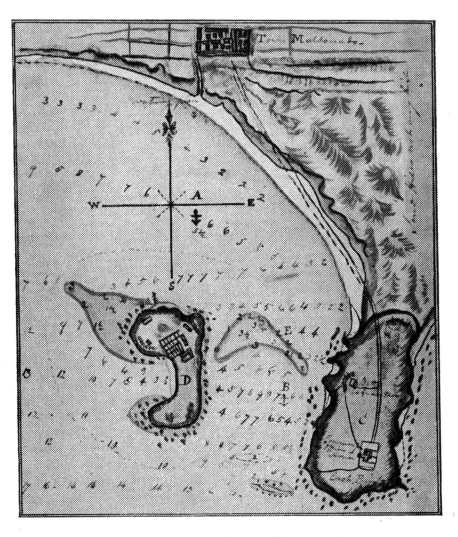

REFERENCES TO THE ABOVE SKETCH OF MALDONADO, &C.

A. Where the Squadron under Sir Home Popham's command anchor'd 30th October, the Island of Gorrita, S. by E., the west point forming the bay, W. by North-East point S.E. ½S, in 6 fathoms water.

B. Where the *Raisonable* [was] anchoring to cover the retreat; if necefsary for our Army to do so, in case of being overpower'd.

C. The low land running out which form the East point.

D. The Island of Gorrita, three batteries and some store houses on it.

E. Where the *Raisonable* touch'd in trying to arrive from A to B and where the *Raisonable* got aground attempting to anchor at B, and in consequence was obliged to go round the Island of Gorrita N.W. pafsage. Near it the *Agamemnon* was lost after in 1809.
.................her track round.

53

Waiting still for the long looked for reinforcement to arrive. We were employed building a battery with our carpenters under the direction of Captain Edward Fanshawe of the Royal Engineers, and destroying those taken from the Spaniards which flank'd the ships. The one we erected was of two guns, in the narrow part of the Peninsula to prevent the enemy, should they attempt to get field pieces down between the sand hills.

The guns and batteries was destroyed on the Island. The Spaniards afsembl'd in great numbers, most of whom were Cavalry, with the intention to prevent our Army from getting supplies of bullocks. Their principal rendezvous was within a mile and half of St. Carlos, but whenever our Army went to meet them they seldom would stand. They had, at several times some smart skirmishes with the Spaniards when our Army was driving the cattle in from the country—in which, tho' we at all times made them run, we lost some fine fellows, among whom a fine young man a Lieut. of the 54th Regiment, who received a mortal wound which occasioned his death in lefs than twenty-four hours, universally esteem'd and regretted.

December 3rd.

This day Commodore Popham superseded by Adml. Stirling.

Arrived the *Sampson*, Rear Admiral Stirling, two India ships and some victuallers, who took the command of the Squadron, &c., in the River Plate. The Commodore haul'd down the broad pendant, and resigned the command. The Admiral would not allow him even a transport to take him home.[1] Sir Home, Captain Wm. King, the First Lieut. and Secretary and other followers[2] obliged to take a pafsage in the *Rolla*, the American Brig detain'd.

Arrived H.M. Sloop *Pheasant*, having on board Major Dean; she was detach'd by Capt. Donally of the *Ardent*, with intelligence that Brigadier Genl. Sir Samuel Auchmuty with a reinforcement was on their pafsage, she parted with them in Latitude 5°00' N., 18°00' West Longitude. Sail'd for the Cape the *Sampson* [64], [H. C. Ship] *Earl Spencer*, [H. C. Ship] *Sir Stephen Lushington*, and *Prevoyant* [Store?] Ship.

Arrived H.M. Ship *Daphne*, with two transports having part of the troops in. This night the *Rolla* sail'd for England with

[1] Popham lived to see Stirling court-martialled for corrupt practices, and placed on half-pay, in 1814. They met as strangers in 1806.

[2] i.e., that portion of the complement which followed the captain from ship to ship, usually including midshipmen, servants, and boat's crew.

Sir Home Popham, Capn. and others above of H.M. Ship *Diadem*.—Adml. Stirling having shifted his flag to the *Diadem*.

Arrived a great number of English ships and vessels richly laden to wait for the port of Monte Video to be open for them.

Arrived His Majesty's Ships *Ardent* [64], *Unicorn* [32], and *Cherwell* [sloop], with the long looked for reinforcement under the command of Sir Saml Auchmuty with the following Regiments as per margin. Every preparation began for the attack. Every day fresh arrivals of English merchant ships. The General and Admiral very busily employed making the arrangement for the attack of Monte Video. On the 13th inst. everything being ready, the troops evacuated the town of Maldonada, viz., the 38th, 47th Infantry, 20th, 21st Dragoons. Embark'd one hundred and thirty horses for the Artillery. At 9 the whole of the ships of war except those mark'd thus *, which remain'd with the neutral ships detain'd in the Bay of Maldonado, the transports and all the English merchant ships proceeded with the Squadron to the place appoint'd to land the Army. At sunset anchor'd near the Isles de Flores.

40th, 87th Infantry.
95th Rifle.
17th Dragoons.
Royal Artillery,
two companies.
Fleet, viz., under the command of Rear Admiral Stirling, viz:—
  Line—*Diadem* [64].
  Raisonable [64].
  Lancaster [64].*
  Ardent [64].
  Diomede [50].*
  Frigates—
  Unicorn [32].
  Leda [38].
  Medusa [32].
  Daphne.
  Sloops—*Pheasant*[16].
  S.S. *Howe*.[1] *Cherwell.*
  Gun Brigs—
  Encounter. Protector.
  Staunch. Rolla.

15th.

The following day at 5 a.m. the Fleet weighed, and again stood up the river. Light winds. Anchor'd near the largest Island. The *Raisonable* touch'd on a sunken rock. In the evening all the boats of the Squadron were sent to the small vessels, ready to land; at the same time the *Raisonable* got under weigh with all the merchant ships, between thirty and forty sail, to anchor to the westward of Monte Video for the purpose of making a demonstration near the South Gate, to draw the enemy's attention from the real place of landing. This morning the sloops and gun vessels took their respective stations close inshore for covering the landing, with the line of battle ships, launches inside them close in. It was about noon when the first Division effected their landing, and by sunset every soldier able to carry arms were on shore. The enemy came down to oppose the landing but, on the launches, gun vessels and sloops keeping a smart fire, they were obliged to retreat precipitately and in great confusion. It was a fine sandy Bay where we landed, about ten miles to the eastward of the town of Monte Video, the ships of the line landing the battering train during the night, and anchor'd off the

16th.

The Landing effected against Monte Video.

Captain Hardyman commanded the boats of debarkation, &c., &c.

---

[1] i.e., Ship-rigged Sloop.

harbour, and the frigates, sloops and gun-brigs alongshore throwing in succours wherever the Army stood in need of them, or any way facilitate their progrefs on their march, and taking off the sick and wounded. The *Raisonable* and frigates anchor'd to the west'd of the harbour to prevent the Spanish gun boats from escaping up the river.

21st.

Lieut.-Colonel Vafsal, 38th Regt., commanded the storming party, who was wounded and died soon after the completion of the afsault.

22nd.
Siege against the town of Monte Video. Brigr.-General Sir Saml. Auchmuty.

The Spanish Army made a sortie from the town in a large body, most of them Cavalry, but were obliged to give way and retreat in great disorder, not above one third got into the town. A great number of them kill'd and wounded. Our Army very near the town. A partial cannonading kept up on both sides.

In the night our Army completed two batteries, and erected a mortar near the citadel and South Gate, near which was judged by the engineers to be the most probable place to make a breach close to the gate. The gun boats in the harbour kept up a good fire on the North Side of the citadel, our batteries commenced and shells thrown occasionally. The citadel kept up a great fire.

23rd.
24th.
25th.

Rain and dirty thick weather, little firing on either side.

A partial firing.

This evening the frigates, sloops, &c., stood in as close as they pofsibly could, and kept up a warm fire, but of no effect as to the damage done. The idea was to draw off their attention, whilst our people were making a battery of six guns, twenty-four pounders, within two hundred yards of the citadel, which was the last and finishing battery. From this day to the 2nd of February almost a constant fire was kept up by our three batteries. The Spanish town and citadel return'd it very briskly.

30th Jany.

The breach appeared conspicuous, but in the night the Spaniards would throw up temporary works to impede our accefs.

January, 1807.

The Spanish fire began to slacken, our batteries kept up a tremendous cannonade, every shot now took away large pieces of the wall, and such a repetition of shot and shells that the Spanish Artillerymen could scarce make their appearance ! The east part of the town, the houses were all in a most wretched condition, and the church was much cut up.

February 2nd.

The breach was considered accefsible for the troops to storm. A company of the 54th Regiment was led on by a promising young Lieutenant of that Regiment, viz., Everat, the

56

PLATE 7.—From a sketch drawn by Lieutenant Walters.   Sketch of the
Town and Harbour of Monte Video Taken by Storm 3rd February, by Major
Genl. Sir S. Auchmuty, Rear Admiral Stirling commanded the Squadron.

References to the Sketch:—A. Citadel.   B. St. Philip, Fort.   C. English Batteries.   D. Spanish Gun Boats.   F. Anchorage, Ships of War.
G. Light House on the Mount.   H. Rat Island.   I. Church in the Centre Town.   JJ. English Army.   LL. Where the breach was made.
M. Where the Gun Boats went after the storm.   N.B.—The red diamond and square [i.e. J.J.] with the lines leading to
S.E. Gate where the breach was made are to represent the storming party assembled in two Divisions.

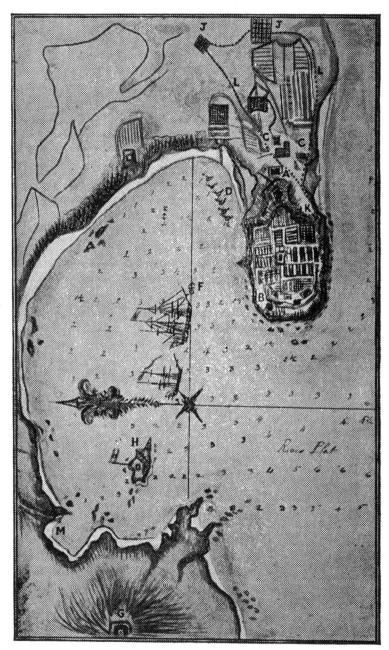

57

Capn of that company being extremely ill at that time, who volunteer'd the forlorn hope, and in a most gallant manner entered the breach on the morning of the 3rd, followed by Lieutenant Colonel Vafsal and the principal part of the 38th Regiment. The boats of the Squadron asembled near the North Gate close to the breach, to be ready to take off wounded, or render such afsistance as was necefsary. I had the command of this ship's boats, under the orders of Capn. Hardyman of the *Unicorn*. Some little time before 2 a.m. the boats reach'd the place near the appointed rendezvous. A constant fire of guns from each side was kept up; the first alarm of the approach of the storming party was announced by their pafsing by and disturbing a number of dogs which is to be found in the vicinity of the town in large bodies, from two to three hundred together. At 2 o'clock most of our soldiers [were] near the breach. When they were discovered by the Spaniards, the flanking batteries near the citadel commenced a most destructive fire. Though before daylight the town, citadel, and forts were all in our pofsefsion, it must be expected that great numbers must have lost their lives in this great enterprise. We had about two hundred kill'd and about three hundred wounded.

*Officers Kill'd
38th Regt.*—
Capn. Mason.
  „ Brownson.
Lieut. Frazier.
Wounded Do. 38th—
Lieut.-Col. Vafsal.
  (since dead).
Captains two.
Lieut's. three.
Afsg. Surgeons two.
Staff—
Lieut.-Col. Brown-
  rigg (since dead).

February 3rd.

At half past 3 the firing ceased on all sides, and at daylight a flag of truce was seen on the citadel, and the Union Jack hoisted on the church in the centre of the town. The boats immediately push'd for the harbour. When we got near the west end of the peninsula, abreast of the twenty-gun ship which the Spaniards had set fire to and deserted, she blew up with a tremendous explosion. About the time of our troops being advanced as far as the church, the troops and many of the inhabitants in the west batteries and all the ships' crews escaped by getting into the gun boats and running acrofs into the Bay to the west'd of Rat Island, and made for Colonia. Upwards of fifty ships and vefsels taken, all in ballast, one twenty gun ship, one of twenty-two and one of ten guns blown up by the Spaniards to prevent being captured at the surrender of the fortrefs. Ships and vefsels of war were taken as per margin, with ten gun boats, each mounting a 24-pounder in the bow, and two boats set fire to but extinguished by our boats before they were destroyed. From this place being taken by afoault, of course the number that fell was

La Paula, 22 guns.
La Fuerta, 22 guns.
La Hero, 10 guns.
La Dolores, 10 guns.
La Paz, 10 guns.
Rayna Louisa,
    French privateer.

chiefly by the bayonet, the breach on the outside at daylight was covered with dead and wounded of the English Army, and in the inside heaps upon heaps of dead were found of the Spaniards, most of whom during the early part of the night of the 2nd were employed collecting and filling up the breach with hides, which were put there to impede the entrance of the British, which afforded the greatest afsistance and facilitated the descending of the afsailants, who soon made their way into the town after having pafsed round towards St. Philip, the north west part of the peninsula, carrying every battery before them. Those of the 38th completed this whilst the Rifle Corps 95th got into the church, having a flat roof, afcended and got on the top of [it] which had the command, being much higher than the citadel, and opened a most destructive fire on them, which were soon silenced, and carried by those brave fellows. This fortrefs had been well defended by the enemy, but in particular by a brave Frenchman, viz., Mourdalls, who commanded the privateer [named] in the margin.[1] His courage, judgment, zeal, and activity in the defence of the town against the English, was such that the Viceroy made him a Colonel and gave him the command of one of his finest Regiments. This poor fellow was kill'd by a bayonet in the citadel. The conduct of Sir Samuel Auchmuty was such that, agreeable to the rule of war any place taken by afsault every thing in it taken is prize property, but notwithstanding, his conduct, lenient as it was, merits the esteem of even those who might lose by it. He gave up all private property, and some public was also claim'd, who generally succeeded in getting it. The fact was, in two day's time the inhabitants open'd their shops. The melancholy appearance wore off by degrees, they soon became cheerful and the whole conduct of the English was such that the Spaniards began to have some attachment towards them, but alas this was not long to exist. Every preparation was now made for our proceeding to the city of Buenos Ayres. Certain intelligence [arriving] of another reinforcement from England, Lieut. Col. Park was immediately appoint'd to command the Light Brigade at Colonia, where that officer had an opportunity of displaying his military talents, which greatly distinguished

February, 1807.

26th inst. General Beresford, Lieut. Col. Park escaped from the Spaniards and came down in the *Cherwell*. The Genl. went to England soon after.

[1] i.e.—In the margin of the previous page. See page 58. This was the *Rayna Lonisa*.

him, as the Spaniards from Buenos Ayres were endeavouring to send troops over to keep back the supplies of stock on the Monte Video side, Colonia being a place situated exactly opposite to B. Ayres. They made several attacks on our force, and [were] as often defeated with immense slaughter on their part, besides great quantities of ordnance and stores taken by Colonel Park in the several actions which took place. The whole of General Sir S. Auchmuty's arrangement appear'd to be ordered with great judgment and executed with ability.

10th May. Sunday.
General Whitelock arrived.

Arrived His Majesty's Ship *Thisbe*, with Lieut. General Whitelock and suite, appointed General-in-Chief of all His Majesty's Forces employed and to be employed in South America. The following day he landed at Monte Video, and took command accordingly. General Auchmuty took command of his Brigade and was paid but little attention to by the new Commander in Chief.

June 14th, 1807.
viz: *Polyphemus* [64].
(Rear Admiral Murray).
Africa [64].
Nereide [36].
Saracen Fly [16].
Camel [Storeship].
Flying Fish.
Haughty [Gun Boat].

Arrived His Majesty's Ships as per margin with a large convoy of transports with the troops so long look'd for. The smallest of those which were already in the river drawing the least water were prepared to shift the troops from the larger ones, to facilitate their getting up the river. The ships of the line struck yards and top masts, and the Admiral made an offer to the General of one third of the seamen of the Squadron to land with and co-operate with the Army, which was only accept'd in part.

21st.

Ships already here under the command of Rear-Admiral Stirling.
Diadem [64].
Raisonable [64].
Unicorn.
Medusa.
Daphne. } Frigates
Thisbe.
Pheasant.
Cherwell. } Sloops
Protector.
Encounter.
Staunch. } Gun
Rolla. } Vessels
Paz.
Dolores.

The troops having all shifted to the smallest transports, the General with Rear-Admiral Murray[1] went on board the *Nereide*, which ship the flag was shifted to from the *Polyphemus*, and the whole expedition got under weigh, and proceeded for the appointed place of rendezvous, where the Army was to be landed. The Marines of the Squadron was sent on shore at Monte Video to garrison it under the command of Colonel Dean, Major 38th R. The whole of the frigates, sloops, and small vessels went up the river. We heard nothing of their progress until 2nd July, some of the transports came down the river with the boats sent up from the Squadron to land the troops, and gave us the following account of them. They effected their landing near Ensernada de Baragon on the 28th

[1] Second-in-command to Stirling. George Murray (1759-1819) had been Nelson's Captain of the Fleet in 1803. It was he who lost the *Colossus* [74], laden with Sir William Hamilton's Collection, in 1798. He had missed Trafalgar and his later career was undistinguished.

60

38th ⎫
40th ⎪
·45th ⎬ Infantry.
47th ⎪
87th ⎪
88th ⎭
95th   Rifle Corps.
9th ⎫
17th ⎪
20th ⎬ Cavalry.
21st ⎭
3 Companies of
   Artillery.
Lieut-General White-
lock's failure in at-
tempting to take
Buenos Ayres, taken
the preceding year by
the 71st Regiment,
200 E.I.C., St.
Helena troops, and
the marines of the
Squadron, 3 of the
line and 2 frigates.
Shame. Shame.
Shame !

July, 1807.

June without lofs or opposition. July 10th the *Rolla* brig came down with dispatches from Admiral Murray to Rear Adml. Stirling. They contained what is but [too] well known, the failure of General Whitelock to his eternal disgrace, with so fine an Army (Regiments as per margin) with great lofs, tho' General Sir Samuel Auchmuty with his Brigade attack'd and carried and took pofsefsion of a battery of twelve guns, the situation of which commanded the Grand Arsenal and the greater part of the city, but by bad arrangement of the Forces being divided, one part being at Reduction, a place but a little way from where they landed, the second part to penetrate the streets of Buenos Ayres, and the third to stay by this battery for supporting those going in. This occasioned the failure.[1]

Immediately after the capitulation took place, Rear Admiral Stirling was ordered with his Squadron to the Cape of Good Hope, with several transports, with two regiments on board, and after a rough pafsage of upwards of three weeks arrived in Simons Bay.

The following orders was ifsued:

Copy.   *Head Quarters before Buenos Ayres.*

                         4th July, 1807.

Sir Samuel Auchmuty to detach the 38th Regt. to pofsefs itself of the Place de Toros and the adjacent strong ground then post itself. The 87th, 5th, 36th, 88th Regiments to be divided into Wings to penetrate the streets exactly in its front, in column of sections right in front; the light battalion to penetrate the street on the right of that leading up from Mr. White's house and the next to it, followed up by the 95th. The left [right?] division of the 95th is to receive its orders from Colonel Park, and left division from General Crawford. Two three-pounders to follow these columns. The 45th to advance in wings right in front, up the two streets beyond the light battalion, the carbiniers to be moved up to cover the two light guns, which will be advanced up the street from Mr. White's house, Head Quarters, and remain with them. Each Officer command'g a Division of the left wing, that is from the 38th to the 87th inclusively, to take care that he does not incline to the right of the right wing, and the light brigade, and 45th to their left; the Cannonade in the centre to be the signal to rush forward and each Division to go if it is pofsible til it arrives at the last square house near the River Plate, of which they are to

[1] See Note 9, page 140.

61

pofsefs themselves, and on the tops of the houses are to form. If they suffer much materially by any internal defence, they are to lodge themselves as far in advance as pofsible. Two corporals with tools to attach themselves to the head of each column, the whole to be unloaded and no firing to be permitted on any account. When the businefs is over the utmost exertion to be used to keep the men collected and form'd. The cannonade to commence 30 minutes past 6 precisely.

OF THE FATAL CONSEQUENCES TO WHICH OFFICERS EXPOSE THEMSELVES, WHO, IN THE DISCHARGE OF THE IMPORTANT DUTIES CONFIDED TO THEM, ARE DEFICIENT IN THAT ZEAL, JUDGMENT AND PERSONAL EXERTION, WHICH THEIR SOVEREIGN AND THEIR COUNTRY HAVE A RIGHT TO EXPECT FROM OFFICERS ENTRUSTED WITH HIGH COMMANDS.

To His Majesty who has taken a most lively interest in the honor and reputation of His Troops, [the recent] failure in South America has [been] a subject of the most heartfelt regret. [It has] been a great consolation to him and [therefore] he has commanded it to be intimated to [his troops], that after the most minute investigation, [His] Majesty finds ample cause for gratification in the intrepidity and good conduct displayed by His Troops lately employ'd on that [expedition] particularly by those Divisions of the Army [at] the town of Buenos Ayres on the 5th July, 1807, and His Majesty entertains no doubt that had the exertions of His Troops in South America been directed by the same skill and energy which have so eminently distinguished his Commanders in other quarters of the world, the result of the campaign would have proved equally glorious to themselves and beneficial to their Country.

By Command of His Royal Highnefs,
Commander in Chief

This intelligence came out by His Majesty's Ship *Leopard* Vice Admiral A. Bertie, [who] arrived on — day of August 1808, and took the command of the Cape Squadron.

Rear Admiral Stirling afsumed the command, tho' he had been appointed to the Command of the Cape station since he left England, but finding Sir Home Popham was in the River Plate, and that Monte Video was to be attack'd by ou troops he repair'd to that River, and there took the comman as mentioned in the preceding pages, and Sir Home oblige to go home in the detain'd American Brig, no ship of wa being allow'd. Trial took place for going to that River (Plate), &c., &c., commenced on his arrival; the result is well known. Admiral Stirling issued orders to detain all ships and vessels belonging to the King of Denmark. The Squadron remain'd in port and little done but putting the Naval Yard in order.

Arrived the sloops, *Otter* and *Sapphire*, the former with a convoy, the latter with Sir Harford Jones, Ambassador for Persia.

Brought the following intelligence that a large expedition had been sent against Island Zeeland under the command of Lord Cathcart and Admiral Gambier, and had bombarded the city and obliged the Danes to surrender, and the whole of the Danish Navy sent to England, sixteen sail of the line, with frigates and sloops, about forty sail.[1]

On the 5th instant arrived a large fleet of Indiamen from India. On the 10th January Rear Adml. Stirling in the *Diadem*, with the *Paz* schooner proceeded for England having the above Indiamen ships under convoy. Captain Rowley assumed the command of the Squadron, who hoisted a Commodore's Broad Pendant, and took the command accordingly. This was very unfortunate for us, we were completed for a five months' cruise, and only the day before we were to sail, when the Admiral altered his mind and determined upon going home, and the Commodore judging the station required his staying in [port], occasioned the *Raisonable's* cruise to be postponed. During this the whole Squadron besides us were cruising.

January, 1808, 20th.
Squadron, viz:
Raisonable [64].
Grampus [50].
Laurel [22].
Otter [16].
Harrier [18].
Cormorant [20].

February 1st.

Sail'd the whole of the Squadron, except this ship, to cruise off Cape La Gullas, where it was expected that a number of Danish East Indiamen would make it homeward bound, being ignorant that England had declared War against them. This was truly annoying to us to remain in at such a time as this.

Arrived from India His Majesty's Ship *Sceptre* [64] with two Danish East Indiaman prizes. She made Cape La Gullas about the time that those two Indiamen did. Only two days before this the *Sceptre* knew nothing of the War, but fell in

[1] This account rather underestimates Lord Gambier's success of September 2nd—7th, 1807. The surrendered ships of the line numbered eighteen, the frigates ten, sloops, &c., fourteen, and gun-boats twenty-five. The reprimanded Sir Home Popham was at Copenhagen as Captain of the Fleet.

The *King George* was taken soon after by *La Manche*, French Frigate.

with the *King George*, a privateer from this place, who inform'd them of the War, and had the good fortune to take them, very richly laden. The *Sceptre* was very leaky, and in a very weak state, altho' a nice ship.

The *Abundance* Store Ship arrived.

The *Abundance* Store ship arrived from England the 18th inst., left England the 29th November last, with the following intelligence: that Rear Admiral Sir Sidney Smith with six sail of the line had been at Lisbon and received on board his ship and the squadron the Queen and Prince of Brazil's and suite, and were gone to Rio Janeiro[1]; also that General Beresford with a small expedition was gone to take pofsefsion of the Island of Madeira.

February 20th. Arrived H.M. Ship *Crocodile* and *Procris* from England.

Nereide arrived from the River Plate in want of a great repair having been in that river since Admiral Murray entered it with the reinforcement.

In consequence of the *Nereide* being very bad in her rigging and wanting caulking all over, and the Commodore wishing the old ship to have a cruise that we might stand some chance with Fortune's Favourite, it was agreed between the Commodore and Captain Corbet that he would shift his broad Pendant to that Frigate during her repair, and Captain Corbet should take the command of the *Raisonable* and cruise. On the 27th inst. Captain Corbet took the Command [of] this ship and the broad Pendant was shifted to the Frigate accordingly, and sailed at 10 a.m., 28th inst.

February, 1808.

Sail'd from Table Bay at noon the 29th, we rounded the Cape, [and] spoke a Portuguese Brig from Mosambique.

Our cruising ground [was] between Cape La Gullas and Hanglip or False Cape. We were in expectation of falling in with some of the homeward bound Danish Indiamen as we well knew they could not have heard of the War being declared in India; however, nothing was seen during the cruise except

March.

H.M. Sloop *Otter*, which we frequently fell in with. On the 31st we rounded the Cape of Good Hope and anchored in Table Bay. At sunset we rehoisted Commodore Rowley's Broad Pendant and Capt. Corbet resumed the Command of

April.

the *Nereide*. On the 2nd April that Frigate sail'd on a cruise in company with the *Otter*. Mr. John Adamson, Surgeon of the *Raisonable* was appointed on the 7th inst. Acting Surgeon of the Naval Hospital at Cape Town. On the 16th arrived H.M. Sloop *Baracouta* from England with Dispatches for India. On the 27th instant we left Table Bay in company with the *Olympia* Cutter. On the evening of the 29th,

[1] See Note 10, page 141.

anchor'd in Simons Bay, found at anchor here H.M. Ships *Nereide*, *Abundance*, and *Otter*. Moored ship; mark bearings, Musamburg N.E. by E., North Battery north, the jetty S.W. by W., the South Battery S. by E. ¾ East, Noah's Ark E. by E. ¾ E.; best bower to the S.W. small bower N.E. Distance from the jetty, half a mile. On the 3rd instant arrived His Majesty's Cutter *Olympia*, and soon after appear'd a ship entering the Bay under Rufsian Colours and a pendant. The *Nereide* got under weigh, and stood for her; sent the *Raisonable's* boat, manned and armed, and took pofsefsion of her. She proved to be the Rufsian Sloop of War, *Diana*, was going on a voyage to explore the N.W. Coast of America, and had a pafs from our Board of Admiralty. Retained her, withdrew the people from her, leaving only a Midshipman on board her, and allowed the Officers to remain in command of her. On the 10th inst. sail'd His Majesty's Ships *Nereide*, *Otter*, and *Cherwell* to relieve the squadron cruising off the Isle of France—*Grampus*, *Laurel*, *Harrier*.

Arrived the *Lord Nelson* and *Doris*, transports from Madrafs, which had spoke on their pafsage to the Cape the outward bound East India Fleet under convoy of His Majesty's Ship *Monmouth*, Rear-Admiral Drury[1]; also that the French Frigate *Piedmontaise* [40] was captured by His Majesty's Ship *St. Fiorenzo* [36] after an action and a running fight of three days. Captain Hardinge fell in the hour of victory. *Fiorenzo* had 35 killed and wounded. The French Frigate 135 killed and wounded. On the 30th instant arrived His Majesty's Ship *Lion* [64] with another outward bound Fleet for India. On the 2nd instant, arrived His Majesty's Ship *Leopard* [50], Vice Admiral A. Bertie, appointed to command the Cape Station. On the 4th the *Laurel* sail'd for to cruise off the Isle of France. The *Raisonable* was ordered to get all ready for sea; [and] on the 17th inst. sail'd from Simons Bay and proceeded on our pafsage to the Isle of France; a very pleasant pafsage. Nothing occur'd worth observation. Made Round Island, commenced cruising to windward of the Island off Port S.E.

On the 3rd the *Leopard* [50] joined Company, on the 6th she parted Company. The *Otter* joined and parted Company occasionally. On the 10th captured the *Pasiphae*, a French Merchant Ship of 600 tons, from the Island of Madagascar

[1] Destined to succeed Sir Edward Pellew as Commander-in-Chief in India.

May.

3rd May.
Arrived *L'Diana*, a Rufsian Sloop, detain'd Capn. Golownins Lieut. Ricord.

1808.
May 20th.
Cruising off Isle of France.

August.

October.

laden with stock bound for Port S.E., having had a very long
pafsage; a great number of the bullocks died, and most of
those remaining were very poor. The *Otter* hove in sight as
we were taking pofsefsion of her. Shifted the prisoners, sent
a Master's Mate with a party of seamen to take charge [and]
sent her to the Cape of Good Hope where she arrived safe.
[On the] 24th the *Sylvia* Cutter joined with Dispatches from
Vice Admiral Bertie. Gave chase to a ship, apparently a
French Frigate. She furl'd her sails when abreast of Port
S.E. in the offing. At that time the *Raisonable* was not seen
by her, being under the High Bambo Mountains, of above the
Harbour. But immediately on her making all sail we gave

Seaflower recaptured.

chase to her. [On the] 27th gave chase to a suspicious vefsel,
the *Sylvia* Cutter in company. From light variable winds at
intervals, inclinable to calm, we did not come up with her
until the following morning when the Cutter brought her
to, proved to be H.M. Brig *The Seaflower*, having been taken by
La Manche [40], French Frigate, off Bencoolen. Manned her
and sent her to the Cape of Good Hope, where she arrived
safe. Gave chase on the 30th to [a] Chafse Maree which got
into Port Lavana. At noon Cape Brabant N. by E.; at 4
rounded the Cape, working up to Port Louis. The following
morning we reconnoitred the Harbour, observed one Frigate,
supposed from reports it was the *Semillante*, having been
patched up and was receiving cargo for some Merchants for
old France. Sent the Master in shore to sound in the *Sylvia*
Cutter. In the evening we commenced our pafsage round to
windward of the Island.

1808. October.

30th. The cutter parted company. On the 3rd November
joined company with the *Otter* who informed us that on the
Sunday morning she gave chase to, and captured, a French
Merchant Ship from Batavia bound for the Isle of France.
Very valuable ship, and it was reported by her crew that
another ship, same description, was expected to be on her
pafsage very soon, being nearly ready when they left it, under
American Colours.

Parted company with the *Otter* and proceeded to Roderigue
to replenish our stock of water and fuel. It being exactly a
dead beat to windward in a Trade wind, and losing more to
the eastward than usual made the pafsage long and tedious.
From the circumstance of the ship being so very light we

did not reach the anchorage of Roderigue until the 10th Novr. Commenced watering and cutting of fuel. Got good supplies of fresh fish, fruit and vegetables, procured a supply of stock turkey and fowls from two French familys who reside here. Being complete with water, &c., on the 19th we sail'd to resume our station off Port Louis. On our pafsage down we captured *La Adventure*, lugger from the Isle of France with people and materials on board her to colonize the Island of Diego Garcia. Not being able to find it they were on their return to Port Louis. We were informed by this vefsel that *La Cannonière* [40] French Frigate, had captured His Majesty's Ship *Laurel* [22] on the 12th Septr. after a most obstinate defence, tho' much inferior to the French ship. The *Laurel* cruising off Port Louis was informed that the ship preparing for sea was the Frigate *Sémillante*, sold to the Merchants and was taking in cargo for Europe, but the sequel was it proved

Cannonière [46] formerly *L'Minerva*. G. Cockburn[2] was Captain of her greater part of the War, prior to the peace of 1802. to be a *forty-gun frigate*. In the evening joined company the *Otter* and was informed that the *Cannonière* and *Laurel*[1] was cruising off Madagascar and had chased some of our small cruisers.

Sent *La Adventure* to the Cape of Good Hope; supplied the *Otter* with water; ran down off Port Louis, the sloop in company; sent in to offer an exchange of prisoners under a flag of truce, no answer could be obtained, the Governor Decaen being in the country. At 3, the French cartel boat

30th. was observed coming out of the Harbour, sent our boat to meet her. The General's answer was that cartels had not been sanctioned by the Admiral Commanding in India for Commodores to appoint them, and that several people whom the Capn. General had solicited for to be exchanged that were taken in the *Pièdmontaise* had been refused and men of colour sent in lieu of them, was his reason for not acceding to the exchange. Being very close in and light variable winds, made all pofsible sail to get an offing. The wind at this time right

1808.
November 30th. in N.W. *Otter* in company. Between 3 and 4 o'clock discovered two strange sail in the N.W., apparently large frigates coming in with all sail set; we being so very close under the

---

[1] Now under French Colours.

[2] George Cockburn (1772-1853) had commanded *Minerve* when Nelson went in her to Elba in 1796 and when Nelson sailed in her through the Spanish Fleet immediately before the Battle of St. Vincent. He lived to take Napoleon to St. Helena and remained there as his jailer until 1816.

high land that the enemy could not see either the *Otter* or *Raisonable*. The weather was in favour of us, as they could not make out the signals which were made to them from the Island. A quarter before nine being very close in whilst in stays, the Batteries fired several shot and threw shells at us, none of which struck us tho' well directed and came near us.

Fell in with *La Manche* and *Caroline* off Pt. Louis.

We tack'd often to keep the weather shore as close as pofsible to prevent the enemy from going between us and it. The enemy in Port Louis and indeed in all the Forts made and repeated a great number of night signals. Observed the two ships to have their wind abreast of Cannonaire Point and heave to, close to each other, and it was supposed had communication. Light airs. A little before 11 they bore up and ran close along shore, the *Raisonable* being so close in obliged them to keep in and it appeared that the headmost one hung for some minutes, there was shoal in that direction; she was soon observed to gather way again. Inclinable to calm. At 12 a Battery abreast of the rear frigate made a private signal which was answered by the van ship. Hoisted our Colours being within range. As we could get no closer, tacked and opened our fire [on] them which they returned, the batteries firing at the same time. This was about midnight. We kept up a brisk fire for half an hour at intervals. At 1 a.m. they entered the port, nor was it in our power to prevent them doing so from their drawing lefs water and the *Raisonable* touching every time we tackd off shore. It was impofsible to prevent them getting in unlefs we had had a frigate with us when we should most probably [have] captured them. We were obliged to carry all sail to get off. Squally, unpleasant weather with hard rain. The following day we ran in off

December 1st.

Port Louis, sent in a boat under cartel colours under a flag of truce, to the buoy to meet one on her way out from Port Louis. We had a very good view of the frigates which proved to be the *Caroline* with a broad pendant and *La Manche* [40], returned from a cruise. Stood off, *Otter* in company; at 7 p.m. parted company, bore up and made sail for St. Denis, Isle of Bourbon. The following day at 6 a.m. made the Cape bearing per compafs S.W.; at 10 saw a strange sail, a ship standing out from St. Denis, all sail set on the starb'd tack, under Arab colours. We immediately gave chase to her and made all pofsible sail, at 10.30 oho tackd, bore up, [and] set studding sails, running alongshore. Very suspicious appearance. At noon she was nearly becalm'd.

December 3rd, 1808.

Very light wind with us, at 3 we hoisted French colours, saw a strange sail S.E. and two more soon after to the north'd—schooners—the chase nearly abreast of St. Rosa. When she came within a mile of that bay, she made a signal for a pilot, with a gun; this was also to alarm the people on that part of the coast, who soon after came running from every direction. There being two batteries in Rosa Bay, [one] of six and one [of] four guns. Soon after she made sail and tackd inshore and ran into the bay and anchored between the batteries, and furl'd her sails. Observed the people on board the Arab filling the long boat with whatever they could get at hand. At 5.15 we took in our studding sails, being nearly within gunshot, shifted our colours and fired a shot at the Arab. Out all boats, sent them armed with all the marines on board her, the batteries firing at the ship and boats. The white people on board the chase had deserted her when the marines got on the quarter deck of the vefsel. They kept up a good fire. The batteries being quite open, they must have been greatly cut up. Besides the fire of the marines we kept eight of the lower and main deck guns playing on them. They found themselves obliged to run from their guns in the batteries and take shelter under the walls and houses. Soon after it fell calm, our people in full pofsefsion and the batteries silenced. They cut the cables and before 8 o'clock, a light wind coming off the land, she was soon towed out [along] side the *Raisonable*. She appeared a fine new ship of about 400 tons, laden with sundry contraband goods, canvafs, &c. The only accident of wounded was the coxswain of one of the cutters lost his arm. She was from Muscat bound to Port Louis or Port S.E. She had two Arabian horses on board her, a present for Capn. General Decaen, Governor [of the] Isle de France. All the papers (log book, invoices, &c.) were either taken by the white people that had deserted her, or destroyed, nor could we obtain the least information [from] the people remaining on board, being all Arabs. Her rigging was much cut, the main yard knocked to shivers. Employed putting her to rights, supplied her with one of our spare topsail yards to replace her lofs of the main yard, shot away. The following day took her in tow and stood down for St. Denis. Variable,

The capture of the *Faza Box*, Arab ship, St. Rosa Bay.

disagreeable, squally weather. It was the Commodore's
intention to reconnoitre St. Pauls, but owing to the badnefs
of the weather we could not venture to approach it. From
the thicknefs of the weather we could only see it at intervals,
altho' close to it. The Commodore at length gave up the
idea of reconnoitring St. Pauls, and we shaped our course
for the Cape of Good Hope. On the 6th we fell in with the
Otter from Madagascar, having watered there. She joined
company and proceeded with us towards the Cape. Saw
some strange ships, supposed last of a fleet of Indiamen, having

parted with their convoy. On the 6th exchanged numbers
with His Majesty's Ship *Powerful* [74]. She telegraph'd [that]
the English [were] at Lisbon, and that the Rufsian Fleet was
sent to England. On the 7th inst. we had a very heavy gale
of wind from the S.W., and west til the 9th. It became
moderate, the wind easterly when we left the *Faza Box* prize
in company with the *Otter*, not having on board at the time
more than three days provision, $\frac{2}{3}$rds allowance. On the 11th
the wind shifted to the eastward, joined company with His

12th instant, noon,
arrived at the Cape
of Good Hope after
an eight months
cruise off Isle of
France.

Majesty's Ship *Powerful* and *Racehorse*, brig. At 9 rounded the
Cape of Good Hope, and the following day anchored in
Table Bay, the Admiral's flag on board the *Caledon*[1], a sloop
of war purchased. Heard from the shore that Captain
Calverhouse, agent for prisoners of war, and his wife were
drown'd in attempting to land in Platenburg Bay, the Admiral
having requested him to go there in a transport to choose out
some of the most likely trees that would answer for the purpose
of the Naval yard, being judged an experienced man. They
were approaching the beach when a most violent surf broke
on the boat, and in an instant the boat was overwhelmed, and
the Captain, his wife, and a Mrs. Bud disappeared. The whole
of the crew got safe on shore ! The body of Captain Calverhouse was never found, but those of the ladies came on shore.
There appeared a little life in Mrs. C. but Mrs. Bud was quite
gone. Being too far distant to procure any medical afsistance
for the former lady, she in a very little time paid the debt

of nature. Came in the *Albion* [74] from India with a convoy
of East Indiamen, having experienced some tremendous
weather in Latitude 9° 0'S. 89° 50'E. On the 29th day of
November last the major part of the convoy parted company,

The Admiral was himself, of courfe, living ashore.

and it was supposed that several were lost; the *Albion* had all her pumps going and baling at every hatchway—threw some of her guns overboard, and [was] obliged to frap the ship amidships. On the 26th inst. arrived H.M. Ship *Nereide* in a truly distrefsed state from the Island of St. Mary's, near Madagascar, her crew having mutinied. A court martial immediately took place on board that ship and lasted three days, when ten of the ringleaders were sentenced to suffer death, nine of whom were strongly recommended for mercy; the following morning the unhappy tenth was executed on board the *Nereide*.[1] Captain Corbet of that ship requested a court martial on himself, which was granted. On the 3rd inst. it commenced, but in consequence of some Documents being wanting, not to be found, the court adjourned till the 6th instant when it was afsembld again. This day the *Raisonable* left Table Bay and went to Simons [Bay], to prepare for heaving down. A strong southerly wind prevailing, we did not arrive there until the 10th inst. Found here His Majesty's Ship and vefsels per margin; heard from Cape Town that Captain Corbet's trial was over, and was sentenced to be reprimanded and admonished.[2] Also that Captain Willoughby's trial had commenced the following day and lasted several days, when he was sentenced similar to Captain Corbet.

16th February, 1809. Lieut. R. Bluett, first of the *Raisonable*, received as per date a letter from Captain Rowley: " Captain Corbet wishes to make Walters (i.e., me) the offer of going with him as 1st Lieut. in the room of Mr. Blight who is invalided; tho' I should be sorry to lose him, I have given my consent if he thinks the offer to his advantage; as the *Nereide* is to sail on Sunday there is certainly not much time to lose in sending an answer." Signed Jos's Rowley. Reply in the negative.[3]

The *Albion* under jury masts and *Powerful* sail'd for England with the homeward bound convoy to call at St. Helena. Captn

February, 1809.
Court Martial on the
Captain of the
Nereide.

Otter, Olympia.
A Court Martial on
Captn. Willoughby.

[1] See Note 11, page 141.

[2] However capable, Captain Robert Corbet had a reputation for cruelty and was extremely unpopular. He was killed in 1810 while commanding the *Africaine* [44] in action with the French frigates *Iphigénie* and *Astrée*.

[3] Walters' refusal was due, one supposes, to Corbet's reputation. Captain Rowley was, no doubt, living ashore, and so conveyed the offer in writing. The words ' if he thinks the offer to his advantage ' were presumably a hint.

Corbet also sail'd with a small squadron to cruise off the Isle of France, consisting of the *Racehorse* and *Caledon*. The *Raisonable*, clearing of all her stores, guns, &c., was haul'd close in to the jetty abreast of the Naval yard. for the purpose of heaving her down; artificers preparing shores for the masts, and outriggers for the support of the lower masts; [the] Master attendant laying the anchors out and getting the purchases ready. The *Pasiphae*, one of our ship's prizes, a ship of about 600 tons, was warp'd alongside of the *Raisonable*. [We] put all the stores on board her, quarter deck, forecastle and main deck guns.

March, 1809.

Simons Bay, Cape of Good Hope.

Raisonable in Simons Bay preparing to heave down. Sent all the lower deck guns on shore to paint and repair their carriages. The ship being perfectly clear and every thing ready on the morning of the 18th inst., began heaving her down to port; found the skin of the ship very good as well as the seams; in fact the only bad part which was discovered defective was the buts and some of the wooden ends.

21st. Arrived the *Cornelia*.

Righted her before sunset. The *Cornelia* [32] from England, going to India, anchor'd in Table Bay. Continued heaving down and righting the *Raisonable*, agreeable to the weather, some days not able to heave down owing to the wind and sea.

April, 1809.
5th. Arrived the *Culloden*.

On the 5th inst. the *Culloden* [74], Vice-Admiral Sir E. Pellew, anchor'd in Table Bay with a part of a convoy from the East Indies[1], having experienced very bad weather in which he had parted with a great many of his convoy.

10th. Arrived the *Terpsichore*.

11th. Arrived the *Nereide*.

Terpsichore anchor'd in Table Bay, one of Sir Edward's squadron. Arrived the *Nereide* under jury masts with the lofs of her main and mizen masts. *Nereide* was reported to have been nearly lost in the tail of that hurricane that the *Culloden* and convoy fell in with, but that active officer, Captain Corbet, collected that scattered part of Sir Edward Pellew's convoy, and had taken them under convoy. He had also purchased small spars to make in lieu of those yards and booms lost when the lower masts were carried away. The fourth day that ship was ready for sea again.

18th. Arrived the *Clorinde* and *Iphigenia*.

[The] *Olympia* cutter came round from Table Bay with a convoy of small vefsels. The *Clorinde* [38] from England anchor'd in this Bay from Table Bay, she brought out the

---

[1] Sir Edward Pellew was on his way home from the East Indies Station, where he had commanded since 1805.

Commifsioners: Shields for the Cape of Good Hope, and Inman[1] for Madras Naval Yards. The *Clorinde* sail'd for India; Sir Edward with convoy for England. The *Iphigenia* joined the Cape Squadron, saild on a cruise off the Isle of France. The *Nereide* and *Iphigenia* arrived and anchor'd in this Bay, the *Sirius* from England to join this Squadron, on the 15th she sail'd for the Isle of France, and the *Raisonable* being for some time the only ship of war in Simons Bay, and nothing near being equip'd for sea, and no provision on board—it being a dark blowing day, wind at N.W. with heavy rain and repeat'd squalls—at 7 p.m. the *Diana*, Rufsian Ship, detained, put to sea, having cut her cables, and escaped out of the bay (the wind being right out)[2] and got off. The Captain and all the officers had previously given their parole to the Commander-in-Chief, but it was judged that they had been prepared for some time to escape, but never having a chance before of the Bay being clear of English vefsels of war.

3rd May. Sail'd *Nereide*, *Iphigenia*. 7th. Arrived *Sirius*.

Sunday, 28th May. Escape of the Rufsian sloop of war, *Diana*, from Simons Bay.

By the beginning of June the *Raisonable* was complete for sea having six months provisions, &c., on board. On the morning of the 15th left Simons Bay to cruise off the Isle of France, to blockade that Island and Bourbon. The following day fell in with, and spoke the Honble Company's Ship *Essex*, one of the convoy from China under the escort of His Majesty's Ship *Lion*; could not board her owing to the very high sea running. Nothing having ocured material, after a pleasant pafsage, we arrived at the Island of Roderigue, for the purpose of compleating our wood and water prior to our blockading Port Louis. On the 11th, having all our wood and water, we left that anchorage and proceeded to the Isle of France. On the 14th joined company *Sirius* and *Iphigenia* [36], the following day parted company with the frigates. On the morning of the 16th made Round Island a few miles to the Northward of the Isle of France, and was joined by His Majesty's Ships *Nereide* [38] and *Leopard* [50], and soon after by the *Otter* sloop. Stood fair for the harbour of Port Louis, enemy's ships then in that port [being] *La Canonnière* [40], *Bellone* [40], and *Laurel* [22], first and latter just returned from a cruise, the other from Europe. Received supplies of provision from the *Ann* transport; the whole squadron was call'd in

15th June.

Arrived at Roderigue. 7th July.

---

[1] He went mad on the voyage and died soon after landing.

[2] The wind, that is, being off-shore.

by the sloop to complete their provision. The *Iphigenia* [36] [had suffered] the lofs of her fore mast, having run on board the *Boadicea* [38], and carried away that ships heel of her bowsprit and fore yard sprang and otherwise damaged, which obliged the *Boadicea* to anchor between Round and Flat Island, to repair her bowsprit, &c. On the night of the 5th August the *Iphigenia* got on shore about two miles to the southward of Cannonaire Point in a bay, with two batteries playing on her. However, it was some time before the Enemy discovered her in that unfortunate situation—prevented by the prudence of her officers putting all lights out, [it] being a very dark night. The enemy kept up a fire on her three hours out of near four, but by great exertion in lightning ship she came off. They hull'd her in several places, two men killed only. The evening of the following day the *Iphigenia* parted company for Bombay to get a new foremast and repair the damages she had sustained in running on board the *Boadicea* and getting aground. On the 5th instant the squadron in the margin being completed with their provisions they took their respective stations afsignd them by the Commodore round the two Islands. The *Cannonière*, notwithstanding, made her escape from Port Louis in one of those very dark nights. The *Raisonable*, with one or more of the sloops [was] watching *La Bellone* [44] being all ready for sea. And fearing in some of those nights she would probably elude our vigilance and to ensure ourselves of a knowledge of the same, our cutters were all provided with paddles, and used to leave the *Raisonable* as soon as it was dark and repair to the *Otter* which was always within gun shot of the outer battery in the entrance of Port Louis. At first they used to fire at her every time she tackd off shore, but being unsuccefsful in not hitting her they at length gave over firing at her. Notwithstanding, we have observed with astonishment how very close she has approached them. Those boats have been paddled within hail of the *Bellone* without being once discovered ! We continued this rigid blockade until the morning of the 17th instant. Being light wind and pleasant weather the *Otter* asked permifson to go round to windward of Round Island, and as it was certain whenever the *Bellone* made her escape it would be with a fresh breeze from the S.E., she was answered in the affirmative, and she crowded all sail and by 10 o'clock that vefsel

Names of the
Squadron:
Raisonable.
Boadicea.
Sirius.
Iphigenia.
Nereide.
Leopard.
Otter.
Sapphir.

Blockading Isle de
France.

was precluded from sight of signal, being the other side of the Island. The *Raisonable*, also, from the appearance of the weather, stood out towards the *Boadicea's* anchorage to inquire by telegraph if her damages were nearly repair'd. To facilitate our communication we were a long way from Port Louis, not lefs than fourteen miles, and about this time (10 and 11 o'clock) the hands being turn'd out to attend some offenders who were to be punished, accordingly, I suppose the only people who were looking towards the port were the men at the mast heads. [The] S.E. trade winds having come on very sudden, together with our ships such a great distance off, that about 11 she was observed by the man at the main-topgall't masthead to have winded, let fall all her sails and slipd. In five minutes time she was clear of the harbour ! with such a crowd of sail as I never before saw. We lost no time in shaping our course after her, and in setting every inch of canvafs that could be set, and the breeze freshened; the *Bellone* also had a fine breeze, she steerd along shore to the westward, and by noon she having reached the N.W. point of the Bay near Black River the wind gradually died away until she was nearly becalmed ! This brought the *Raisonable* up with her, but about half an hour after 12 o'clock we got into the same light variable wind, not above two gun shot length from her, indeed we were so near to her that we beat to quarters and expected to have been alongside of her in at most [a] quarter of an hour. During the whole of this time signals had been made and repeated to the *Boadicea* to chase ships in view, and make all pofsible sail; it was enforced with guns. Notwithstanding, it was 3 o'clock before that ship made sail. The enemy in Port Louis, always ready to afsist the ships, and very clever in suggesting a stratagem to elude us; the *Laurel* which had been previously lying with her yards and top-masts struck, was now while we were yet in sight winded, having her head pointed out of the entrance bending sails and in every respect likely to come out that evening. Commodore Rowley being somewhat displeased in the *Boadicea* protracting her commencing the chase, altho that ship was nearing the *Bellone* with a fine breeze, and it was generally supposed we should have had her as a prize that night if the *Boadicea* had been permitted to have stood on. Notwithstanding, her signal made was to repair off Port Louis, from which circumstance

La Bellone's escape from Port Louis.

Light variable winds, and sometimes fresh. *Raisonable* in chase of *La Bellone*. Shaping her course for the Bay of Bengal. Several times within long chase guns, but ultimately she got off after several days' chase.

the *Bellone* escaped. However she parted company accordingly, and we pursued the enemy's frigate *Bellone*. [The] *Raisonable* continued in chase of the *Bellone* all the night of the 17th, Commodore Rowley judging that the intention of the enemy was to have communication with the Island of Bourbon, as *La Caroline*, French frigate had just arrived at St. Pauls from a cruise in the Bay of Bengal with two valuable prizes, English East Indiamen.[1] Took in all the studding sails and kept under all plain sail, going with the wind free on the larboard quarter. During the night we observed that most beautiful scene, a volcano; as it was a very dark night it appeared delightful. A little before daylight observed some false fires and rockets made. Supposing ourselves about abreast of Saint Pauls, we of course, concluded it to be the *Bellone* making private signals to the *Caroline*, nor was we much out in our conjecture, for at daylight the *Bellone* was discovered right a head of us under her topsails and top-gallant sails, and for certain was going to have communication with the *Caroline* which was not above five or six miles from us in

Port St. Pauls; she soon was under a crowd of sail, and the *Raisonable* set every sail that would draw. A fine breeze. We drew so much on her about 10 o'clock that we were about to shorten sail expecting to be alongside of her in lefs than a half an hour; in this flattering way were we jaded by the inconstant and very partial wind, at times allowing us to come within almost gun shot and then leaving us becalmed and allowing the *Bellone* to increase her distance to ten or twelve miles. However, we continued the pursuit till the night of the 20th inst. when we lost sight of her; it was evident by the course she had steer'd she was going to cruise in the Bay of Bengal. We form'd our course for Saint Pauls as it was Captain Rowley's intention to reconnoitre that port, but owing to adverse winds we did not arrive off it until the

24th inst. when we observed in that roadstead *La Caroline* [40], French frigate, and two Indiamen prizes, [and] several small vefsels. We stood close in and obferv'd they were moord head and stern as close under the batteries as they could be, the frigate apparently ready for sea, her prizes with their yards and topmasts struck. I rather think that Commodore

[1] The H.C. Ships *Streatham* and *Europe*, taken on 31st May when on their homeward passage from Bengal River.

76

Rowley from that moment had determined to attack the place with the squadron. Two vefsels were seen to the S.W. of us about 11 a.m., which proved to be the *Otter*, sloop of war, in chase of a vefsel which she captured, *L'Agile* a French merchant brig from Europe bound to the Isle of France, which had been previously taken by His Majesty's Ship *Nereide*, and was on her pafsage to the Cape of Good Hope in charge of a Master's Mate; they came within two days' sail of it when the major part of the *Nereide's* men joined the French prisoners[1], and mutinied, and killed the prize master, and was on their return to any port they could reach in either

Recapture of *L'Agile,* brig.

of the Islands, but the *Otter* in quest of the *Raisonable* was fortunate enough to fall in with her. Notwithstanding, the mutineers made their escape in her boats, [and] altho' pursued by the *Otter's* boats, they got safe on shore. The following day we fell in with the *Nereide*, and we all proceeded off Port Louis. That active and zealous officer, Captain Corbet was detached with the *Otter* and *Sapphire*, sloops, to Roderigue for the purpose of requesting Lieut. Colonel Keating to afsist us with what numbers of troops he could spare for the attack of Saint Pauls; that officer having been sent by the Government of India with about six hundred troops, principally of his own regiment, the 56th, and some•native Infantry. With the greatest celerity, the Colonel acceded to it, and volunteerd to command them in person, which was readily accepted, and on the evening of the 18th September, the *Nereide* [36], *Otter* [18], and *Wasp* (Company's schooner) joined the *Raisonable*, and *Sirius* [36] off Port Louis with about four hundred troops

September.
Lt. Colonel Keating and troops came down from Roderigue in the *Nereide* for the attack of St. Pauls.

on board. The Colonel immediately waited on the Commodore, and arrangement was planned that evening. The following day the squadron having all afsembled for the purpose of the attack ran down to leeward of the Island, off Black river, for the purpose of putting the troops and marines on board the *Nereide*, that ship having been appointed to land the whole detachment. Tho' rather crowded, it was to prevent any alarm being made by the inhabitants, and as the near approach of our ship was never noticed, it allowed the troops to be disembarked without any opposition, and I may say without the enemy having the smallest knowledge of it, as the *Boadicea* [38] had been off the Port of Saint Paul's since the arrival of

---

[1] See Note 12, page 142.

the *Caroline* in that port. It is my opinion that a more clever man could not have been found or selected than the gallant Corbet, the result of the succefs verifies the same, and which has been acknowledged by all who knew the circumstance. The squadron kept so close in with the West part of the Isle of France, laying to, sending the marines of the squadron to the *Nereide* with all the barges and cutters, which were hoisted up to temporary davits fixed round that ship, and such was the dispatch that by sunset every thing was prepared for proceeding for the place of destination. I rather think that General Decaen must have thought that it was our intention to have made a descent on that Island by our hovering about that place; however he must have soon been undeceived, as the moment it became dark the *Raisonable* bore up with the squadron [named] in the margin. It was planned as follows: That we should go under easy sail about three knots per hour, as that would take us about half way between the Island of Mauritius and that [of] Bourbon by noon the following day; and so we had steerd for the east point of the latter Island until we made out the land from the mast-head, which was about 10 o'clock a.m. (owing to its being very hazy and which was greatly in favour of the expedition). As the moment we made it out we altered the course to N.W.—St. Pauls, the port we were going to, being on the north part of Bourbon. We ran on until sunset, never in sight or [so] close that the enemy could make out what we were. A little after dusk the squadron hove to, and, soon after, the *Boadicea* joined, which ship had been blocking up the *Caroline* and her prizes, as we were aware that it was Decaen's wish to get them in to any port of the Isle of France. Captn. Corbet and Colonel Keating came on board to wait on the Commodore previous to the attack, to consult; each ship of the squadron having their orders how to act in case the enemy's vefsels should attempt to get out of the Bay. All of them had their stream cable out of the gun-room ports, and the *Raisonable*, a bower cable out of [her] stern port. Soon after, the Colonel returned with Captain Corbet to the *Nereide*, which ship bore up for Point Galet, the point with Saint Denis which forms the east arm of the Bay of St. Pauls. Very light wind all the first watch; by midnight the *Nereide* had not run above one third of her distance towards Galet point. But soon after daylight, [when] we were about to

1809. 19th Sept.

Raisonable.
Sirius.
Nereide.
Otter.
Wasp, Schr.

Boadicea join'd.

Exact account of the force under the command of Lieut. Colonel Keating:—
368 (56th Regiment and Native Inf.).
100 Seamen.
136 Marines.
——
604 total.

telegraph to know if the troops were disembarked, that ship was laying within a quarter of a mile of the beach, sails all furl'd, and it is believed that she had never been discovered by the enemy from her anchoring to her making sail from it. Before we had time to hoist the second number, she made the whole at once, as follows " troops on shore and near the first battery." At that moment the frigate's anchor trip'd, and she was in [i.e., under] a crowd of sail. [She] joined the squadron and took her station in succefsion in the line, and sent the boats to their respective ships, with a celerity peculiar to the gallant Captn. Corbet. Very soon after, the report of several guns were heard, and about 6 o'clock we had the pleasure of observing the Union Jack planted on the first or Eastmost battery—a great succefs in such a short time, not more than two hours [having] elapsed from the debarkation of the little force, which consisted of two companies of the 56th Regiment, one company of Native Infantry about 300; the Marines about 180; seamen to act as Artillery, 150; in all about 600 men. This gallant little army was commanded by Lieut. Colonel Samuel Keating, the senior officer of the Marines, the sen'r. Lieutenant of the *Sirius*, senior Captain of the 56th (acting as Major) and the seamen under the command of Captain Willoughby the Com'r. of the *Otter* sloop. It appeared that the guns that was last heard was from the Battery, which had been carried by our army by surprize, and they, [the enemy], having fled without having time to spike or dismount the guns, our force was immediately able to commence firing on the second battery. As this place was considered the Gibraltar of both these Islands, it is the more to be wondered at, that we should have succeeded in reducing it in such a short time. However, it will be necessary to observe that the fortification of the Bay of Saint Pauls—which is in a crescent with water deep enough to admit a ship of the line close in with the shore, having a chain of batteries consisting of seven, with regular works, mortars, and magazines, with upwards of one hundred pieces of cannon mounted, calibres from 32 to 18 pounders—our squadron could not approach the anchorage of the enemy until the position of our troops was ascertained, having lost sight of them in their

21st September.
Reduction of St. Pauls in the Island Bourbon.

79

Commodore Josias
  Rowley's Squadron
  in the attack on the
  Isle Bourbon and the
  shipping in St. Pauls
  Bay.
Raisonable.
Boadicea.
Sirius.
Nereide.
Otter.
Wasp, schooner, E.I.C.
  Cruiser.

Attack of St. Pauls in
  the Island of Bourbon

advance towards [it]. In this suspense we remained for upwards
of 20 minutes, before we heard any firing, the squadron all
ready to stand in the moment that we could commence firing
on the enemy's ships clear of our troops. It was known by
the Union Jack being on the third battery la [*Neuf*] that three
out of the number were in our pofsefsion, but the situation
of our troops was about this time, 7 o'clock, the most difficult—the centre grand battery, abreast of the town of St.
Pauls, being the place of retreat for the enemy's troops, who
had deserted the three first batteries which were carried by
our troops. But such was their consternation on the approach
of the afsailants that they never made a stand to observe who
or what number they had to contend with until they arrived
at the centre battery; and by that time our force had advanced
near enough to observe what the enemy's intention was.
They were seen (by the officers sent to reconnoitre their
position) in great numbers, drawn up between the town and
the battery. Colonel Keating determined to attack immediately.
Captain Hanna of the 56th Regiment was ordered to be ready
with the third column for the support of Captain Imlack,
who had been detached with the second column, composed
of 142 of the 2nd Battalion of the 2nd Regiment of Bombay
Native Infantry and twelve Europeans, to take pofsefsion of
the 3rd battery deserted by the enemy. On his way thither
he fell in with and was opposed by the entire force of the
French, who had concentrated and taken up a very strong
position behind a stone wall, with eight brafs field pieces,
6-pounders, upon their flanks. This post was instantly
charged in the most gallant manner by that Officer and his
men.

  The enemy however maintained their position and Captain
Hanna of the 56th Regiment was ordered to proceed with the
third column to Captain Imlack's support, who charged and
took two field pieces from the enemy. The action now became
warm, but never doubtful. The enemy being reinforced from
the hills and having also received 110 troops of the line from
the French Frigate *La Caroline,* and the squadron not being
able to stand [in] to the support of our troops from their movements being endangered by their fire, except at intervals—
which was always taken advantage of—Captain Willoughby
was directed to spike the guns of the batteries in our pofsefsion,

and with the seamen to man the third battery, which commenced a very heavy fire on their shipping. By this arrangement, Captain Forbes, who, with the reserve, had covered those batteries, was enabled to advance against the enemy, who after an honourable resistance was compelled to give way; their remaining guns being carried by that excellent officer. A sufficient number were ordered to act as light troops, and to pursue the enemy, whilst the 3rd column with part of the reserve advanced against the 4th and 5th batterys La Prira and La Cassvue, which fell into their hands without opposition and whose native fire was turn'd upon the enemy's shipping. By half past eight o'clock the town, batteries, magazines, eight brafs field pieces, 117 new and heavy iron guns of different calibres, and all the public stores were in our pofsefsion, with several prisoners.

7-30 a.m.
Lieut. Walters 2nd *Raisonable* took possession of *La Caroline* Frigate.

The instant the squadron perceived that the object in landing had succeeded, and that they could with safety to the troops stand in effectually, they immediately anchor'd close to the enemy's shipping, which after a short firing, surrendered. The entire of the batteries being destroyed and the town completely commanded by our squadron, the troops were reimbarked by 8 o'clock the same evening. The above is an abridgment of Lieut. Colonel Keating's report to the Commander-in-Chief of the Army at Bombay of the operations relative to the reduction of St. Paul's.[1]

22nd instant.

On the following day in the evening the enemy appear'd in some force upon the hills, and a heavy column was observed advancing from St. Denis, which I since understand to have been under the immediate command of General des Brusleys. The Commodore and Colonel agreed upon the propriety of landing a sufficient force to destroy all public property, and accordingly the Marines, with a few soldiers, under Captain Willoughby, was ordered upon this service, who effectually burnt an extensive Government store of considerable value; the remaining stores were only saved from some doubt existing respecting their being public property. On the morning of the 23rd the entire force was put into the boats to reland and attack the enemy whose retreat however during the

---

[1] It is almost a literal transcript in parts. The subsequent paragraphs are the author's own.

night to St. Denis prevented the necefsity of any further debarkation.

The Commandant, St. Michel, being disposed to enter into negotiations, with the concurrence of Commodore Rowley, the preliminary articles were drawn up, a copy of which follows. The Commandant accompanied the Colonel on board the *Raisonable*, where they were signed, subject to confirmation or rejection of the Commander-in-Chief, General des Brusleys. On the 24th all the remaining public stores were delivered over by the head of the police, and fatigue parties from the squadron and troops were ordered to embark them on board the Honourable Company's recaptured ship *Streatham*, which, together with the *Europe* were placed under the orders of their former Commanders, From the 25th to the 28th the whole of the guns, &c., were finally destroyed, the guards continuing to mount regularly in the town for the protection of the inhabitants and their property.

By the Articles of agreement, a mutual suspension of arms was immediately to take place; public property to remain in pofsefsion of the English. The English not to be prevented from attacking any other part of the Island, either by sea or land. Three days given for ratification by General des Brusleys.

In consequence of the sudden death of General des Brusleys,[1] a further delay of five days was granted.

A list of ships and vefsels captured and destroyed in the road of St. Paul's, Isle of Bourbon, 21st December, 1809.

La Caroline, frigate of 46 guns (28 long 18-pounders, eight 36-pound carronades) and 360 men. Commanded [by] M. Ferretier, Lieutenant de Vaisseau.

Grappler, brig, pierced for 16 guns, 11 on board, six 18-pounders mounted; three long six-pounders in the hold.

Merchantmen captured and destroyed:—

Streatham, ship of 30 guns, and 819 tons, partly laden with saltpetre, the rest of her cargo landed.

Europe, of 26 guns and 820 tons ditto...

La Fanny, brig of 2 guns and 150 tons laden with rice and corn.

Trois Amis, of 60 tons, laden with slaves and rice.

Le Creole, schooner of 50 tons, in ballast.

1809.
24th September.

Capitulation of
St. Pauls.

La Caroline, F. Fgate.
Streatham } E.I. ships.
Europe
Fanny, Brig.
Trois Amis, Schooner.
Creole, Schooner.
Several destroyed.

Ships captured at
St. Pauls.

[1] He had shot himself.

82

Three vessels, names unknown, destroyed.

One ship, name unknown, burnt on the stocks.

(Signed) Jos. Rowley.

Officers and Seamen
killed and wounded
of the Squadron.

A return of killed, wounded and missing belonging to His Majesty's Ships under the command of Josias Rowley, Esq., Captain [of] His Majesty's Ship *Raisonable*, in action with the enemy, St. Pauls and its vicinity, Island of Bourbon, 21st September, 1809.

KILLED:

Raisonable............... 1 able Seaman, 1 private Marine.

Boadicea .... 1 private Marine.

Sirius.................... 2 private Marines.

Nereide .... 1 able Seaman.

Otter .... 1 private Marine.

Total, 7.

WOUNDED:

Raisonable............... 1 Lieutenant, 1 able Seaman.

1 Lieut. R. Marines.

2 private Marines.

Boadicea .... 1 Lieutenant of R. Marines.

1 Corporal, 2 privates.

Nereide .... 1 Corporal, 4 private Marines.

Otter .... 1 able Seaman.

Sirius.................... 2 private Marines, 1 ordinary Seaman missing.

Total, 18 and 1 missing.

(Signed) Josias Rowley.

Officers and men killed
and wounded of the
force under the Com-
mand of Colonel
Keating.
56th Regiment.

A return of killed, wounded and missing of the force under the command of Lieut. Colonel Keating, 22nd September, 1809.

Total: 15·killed, 38 wounded, 3 missing.

NAMES OF OFFICERS WOUNDED:

Royal Marines—Lieut. J. R. Pye, 2nd Lieut. Mathew Hardon.

Second Battalion—2nd Native Infantry, Lieut. Grant, Sabidar Shaik Solomon.

(Signed) Henry S. Keating.

Thus was completed in the run of a few days, the ruin of a port which had for a series of years sheltered the enemy's cruisers, and it is well known that ships of the line and frigates, which have ventured in on trial have been very glad to haul off and get safe out after experiencing great damage nor do I think we should have succeeded in any other method of attack.

I have now to return to the *Raisonable*, and give account of the squadron from the place I left them, which was lying to, waiting to discover the position of our troops on shore, which was then about 7 o'clock, and it was known that three of the batteries were in our pofsefsion and at length we observed the Union hoisted on the grand centre battery. At the same time all the other batteries were deserted and taken pofsefsion, and manned by our seamen acting as artillery with the force on shore. The squadron immediately bore up and stood in for the shipping. The batteries kept up a smart fire on the frigate and Indiamen prizes. The advanced ships commenced a most destructive fire and in a very little time they all surrendered and struck their colours as per list [on previous page].

Thus was executed in lefs than four hours by the superior skill and judgment of a few clever men, plans what treble the force would have failed in under inferior commanders, than those employed on this succefsful expedition !

I was sent by Commodore Rowley to take pofsefsion of the *Caroline* Frigate, prize to the squadron. On my coming on board her she was in the greatest confusion, which is usual almost to find it the case. The moment they find that they have surrendered they make for the spirit room. I do not censure the French more than any other countrymen, for it is just the same if an English ship is captured by the enemy. I found on board that ship the senior lieutenants of the *Sirius* and *Nereide*, both of whom had been sent nearly at the same time to take pofsefsion of the frigate; however, as I was sent by the Commodore, I directed them to go to the afsistance of the *Europe* and *Streatham*, Indiamen, their bow and quarter mooring being either shot away, or cut, by which they were striking—which they did. It was about 8 o'clock when I got on board *La Caroline*, and it was near 10 before I could get the prisoners and their baggage away; notwithstanding all the boats of the squadron were employed in this service. It will be necefsary for me to explain [of] what this baggage consisted. As in an English Ship of War, every seaman can carry all his traps with him. However, I think it would have puzzled the strongest Frenchman among the crew to have carried his [share of the] clothes and goods which they claimed as their property at three turns.[1] The way those ships managed as cruizers when they get into the Bay of Bengal or the [rendezvous?] they intend to cruise near is as follows. The first thing that they look out for is the country coasting vefsels, which they detain as prizes, and keep for two or three days, perhaps all the time prompting and endeavouring to gain by artifice an account of what Ships of War they have met on their voyage; those they left in port; what Indiamen were there, what cargo are they taking in and when are they expected to sail. And should they not succeed in gaining the intelligence they want to gain, probably they will be put down in the dark hold with little food until they promise to give them a faithful account; when they are informed if they do that they shall have their vefsel again. This has a wonderful effect, most probably. They have learnt every particular and the poor fellow is under the idea that he will get the vefsel as she was [at] the time she was taken pofsefsion. It is probable, [however, that] they will run her to the very opposite and most distant port so that the cruise will be expired before the fellow can give any intelligence of the frigate being in that quarter. And when they allow the vefsel to part company, all the boats are sent to take [from her] all private Trade and such part of the cargo as they can conveniently get at, besides all the moveables. And perhaps they may during a cruise serve two or three dozen vefsels in this manner. This is what they call a privilege for their seamen, but in plain English it is call'd plunder ! However, by this method they elude the vigilance of our ships of war in the Indian Sea, and are seldom or ever seen by any of them, and by this very method those Indiamen were taken by the *Caroline*. It was known long ere she fell in with them that they were much cumbered and consequently could make but a poor defence. But to proceed. As to clearing the frigate of her prisoners, I found after most of them had taken their bags with them that the hammock netting was still full, fore and aft, with immense large bags of this plunder, consisting of pieces of the best China Nankeen, Dimity, and Calico. There was enough by a fair distribution to give every man in the squadron

[1] i.e., in three trips.

a jacket and trousers; which was done, or nearly so. I had only two boats' crews with me at the time and two midshipmen, and the ship tho' [in] smooth water, at times tail'd in with stern towards the beach and struck at times. That active, clever man, Captain Corbet, bent on hawsers to the bower cable which the *Nereide* was then riding by, until she was within a half cables length of *La Caroline*, and then let go the *Nereide's* other anchor, sent the end of her stream cable to us, and hove us off into deep water, and sent the end of the cable slip'd from the *Nereide* to the prize, by which we were a half a cable's length further off shore, in 12 fathoms water. All this was done in less than 40 minutes. I was informed that the *Boadicea*[1] would send on board another end of a cable, which would moor the *Caroline*; that ship was just as near to us as the *Nereide* was when I received her cable, but such was the difference between the two ships in giving afsistance that I did not receive the *Boadicea's* cable until the next morning. During the night a light wind came off the Town, and the conflagration of the public store set fire to, that I was somewhat alarmed that some of the sparks might light about the prize, and perhaps set fire to her. However, nothing occurred during the night, and the following morning I was succeeded in the command and charge of *La Caroline* by Lieut. Bluett, he being the first Lieut. of *Raisonable*. It is usual on those occasions for the Senior Lieut. of [the] Commodore's ship to be sent in the first Ship-of-War taken, with a view to promotion. However on my return I became Senr. Lieutenant, being before, second. I now had to afsume [the duty of] principal executive Officer, and at this period it was

Employed with fatigue and working parties from the Squadron in putting the cargo found on shore on the *Streatham*, and destroying the guns and batteries, &c., at St. Pauls.

far from being considered a desirable situation. The Commodore and Captain with the Colonel were all on shore from daylight in the morning till sunset, and many a day I have been up from 2 o'clock in the morning till 11 at night, and the greater part of the day on deck. Notwithstanding I found, as in general is the case, that the more I [had] done, the more was expected to be done. I found Captain Rowley quite altered almost the second day. I had been with him upwards of four years from Junior to Senior Lieut. and always on the best of terms. However, I found him peevish, very seldom in a good humour, and whatever was done in his absence was

[1] Commanded by Captain John Hatley.

86

found fault with, notwithstanding I had been double diligent in my endeavouring to please him, and was ever ready to make an allowance that it was occasioned by something not going on on-shore as he wished. But a continuance of it *at last* made me suppose that he was not pleased with my arrangement. However, I was determined if pofsible to execute my duty so as to give satisfaction. But I must own I found him as different a man as could be, to that he used to be when I was one of the junior Lieuts. Finding it so, I must own I was not a little chagrined, but made the best of it; I wishd much to have pleased him, but trusted it would be over as soon as the prize goods was taken off and stowed on board the *Streatham*, or at the farthest when we got to sea again. From this anchorage, *Nereide*, Captain Corbet, sail'd with dispatches for the Cape of Good Hope on the 1st instant, and by the 5th everything being on board the *Streatham*, which ship was to proceed to England. In the evening the *Otter*, Captain Willoughby, left this anchorage with the *Caroline* Frigate; *Streatham*, Indiaman recaptured, *Fanny*, *Grappler*, and *Trois Amis*, prizes; and the following day the *Raisonable*, *Europe*, recaptured Indiaman, and the *Creole*, schooner, sail'd from St. Pauls for the Island of Roderigue, with the Detachment of the 56th Regiment and Native Infantry on board the *Raisonable* and *Europe*. Owing to strong winds and a lee current, together with the *Europe's* tardy conduct in making sail, we did not reach the Island of Roderigue till the 22nd instant, having parted company with the *Europe* two days, but fell in with her before we made the Island. Disembarked the troops, and commenced watering and wooding of the ships. We received large supplies of most excellent fish and some vegetables from the cabbage tree. The latter part of this month a transport arrived from Madagascar laden with bullocks; received for the squadron and for the use of the *Raisonable* about one half of his cargo. Being all complete with wood and water, as well as the *Europe*, we saild from Roderigue. Soon after, we parted company with the *Europe*, which proceeded on to India, and we went for our old cruising ground off Port Louis. On the 3rd instant joined company with the *Iphigenia* [36] off Port S.E.; on the 4th reconnoitred Port Louis, found the only Ship of War in that port was the *Laurel*, two sail in sight to leeward and one

1st October.

Raisonable's arrival at Roderigue.

1st November.

to northward, which proved to be His Majesty's Cutter, *Olympia*; and the vefsels to leeward the *Creole* schooner (tender) and *Diadem*, transport victualler, from the Cape of Good Hope. Soon after, they joined company with us. When the Midshipman coming from the tender came on board he informed us that the only vefsel of war in Port Louis was the *Laurel*, and that on the morning of the 3rd inst. the *Confiance*, formerly the *Cannonière* was mifsed from Port Louis by His Majesty's Ship *Boadicea*, which ship immediately went in quest of her. She was purchased, it was reported, by some French Merchants from this Government, to take home a cargo of India Prize Goods. The *Laurel* was reported to be loading with a similar cargo. The *Boadicea* joined company again having seen nothing of the *Confiance*. We kept off and on Port Louis, every port having Ships of War blockading it, two frigates off Port S.E., one off Bourbon, and two sloops and *Raisonable* off Port Louis. We were certain that the enemy's squadron must soon return to one of those places, and nothing of any consequence took place worth mentioning in this narrative till, on the 18th, the *Harriett*, an English cartel [arrived] from Calcutta with one hundred and twenty French prisoners on board, most of whom were officers which had been taken in India by our cruisers in that quarter, some belonging to *La Cannonière*, *Manche*, *Laurel*, and *Piédmontaise*. We detained her that day, the following evening she was permitted to go into Port Louis. On the evening they [the ships named in the margin] were detached for the Seychells, in quest of the long looked for French squadron, as sometimes they have been known to shelter there when their ports about these Islands have been watched so close as to prevent any chance of their being able to get in with their prizes. In the morning discovered two sail off The Cape Brabant, which proved to be His Majesty's Ship *Boadicea* and a prize brig from the Isle of Bourbon, being the same enemy's brig that escaped from Port Louis on the night of the 9th instant, laden with ordnance stores for Bourbon, which was safe delivered, and was on her return to Isle de France where she was captured. At 11 the *Boadicea* joined company, her foremast being sprung. Both ships hove to, [and] we sent all our shipwrights on board to afsist in fishing it. At this time there was a French brig laden with India goods all ready for sea and then in the

25th instant joined
company.

Sirius.
Iphigenia.
Sapphire.
21st instant.

entrance of the Harbour, ready to take advantage of a dark night or the distance of ships of war from the Island. Captain Rowley enquired where the Tender was, which had gone inshore some time since and was almost out of sight. We had drifted a long way out from the port, owing to a fresh S.E. wind, having been lying to by the *Boadicea* ever since she joined company for the purpose of being close to her to afsist with materials as well as artificers in fishing her mast. Captain Hatley dined with the Commodore, and at sunset, finding we were such a great distance off, he ordered Capt. H. to stand to the S.W. while the *Raisonable* would work up to the S.E., that in case the brig should venture out during the night, that she would be seen either by the *Boadicea* to south'd, and westward by the *Creole*, Tender, in the N.W., or by the *Raisonable* in N.E.; from Port Louis. It was judged for certain that she would attempt it between 5 and 6 o'clock, each ship made sail and set everything that would draw, and by 10 o'clock the *Raisonable* wore and hove to, close in with Port Louis, so that if she had not come out before that period she would not be able to affect it that night. In this position the *Raisonable* continued all night; daylight came and we observed that the brig had escaped from Port Louis during the night, and that the *Boadicea* not being in sight from the mast head it was judged that she had got sight of her, and was in pursuit of her. At 4 p.m. observed a ship to leeward, which proved to be the *Boadicea* per signal. The following day at noon she joined company with us. On her Captain coming on board, we were informed it was as suggested, that they captured her on the preceding morning at 4 o'clock, after a chase of upwards of four hours, and had sent her to the Cape of Good Hope. It is to be wondered at, that under the circumstances above pointed out, that the officers of the *Boadicea* should object to the *Raisonable's* sharing, but so it was, and altho' she was condemned at the Cape as a joint capture, yet they were determined to try it again in England. However, after a mature deliberation and taking the advice of some lawyers they gave up the idea, and agreed that the case of the two ships should be drawn out and sent to England to be laid before one of the most eminent men of the Admiralty Court, for his decision thereon, which settled the affair finally. I am happy to say it was given in our favor,

22nd instant.
The capture of the *Margueritta*, a French Merchant Brig bound to Europe from the Isle of France.

1809.
December.

and I think it would have been most unjust had it not, for I am certain if it had been the *Raisonable's* lot to have captured her in lieu of *Boadicea*, we should never [have] objected for a moment [to] her sharing.

The *Otter* was seen on the evening of the 26th and joined company the following day. [She] brought intelligence that a large expedition from England was gone against Holland,[1] the object in view was to get the ships of war laying in the port of Flushing, which place was taken, but the French Fleet having removed to Antwerp, and a sicknefs soon after prevailing in our Army, that place was evacuated and the ultimate end in view given up, and we withdrew our Fleet and Forces.

We were also informed that *La Caroline*, French Frigate taken at St. Pauls, was commifsioned by Captain Corbet of His Majesty's Ship *Nereide*, and that Captain Willoughby of the *Otter* was appointed to that ship, acting post. She parted company at noon to recall the *Leopard* from to windward. Extremely hot and sultry weather and frequent calms. On the 20th instant we had a fresh breeze; the signal was made

at the several stations that several of the enemy's vefsels were to windward, which we supposed to be the *Leopard* and *Otter* coming down. In the evening the former joined company with us off Port Louis. On the following day, Sunday, we were employed delivering our provisions to her (as we were going into the Cape, to revictual and refit the ship) except as much as would just last us into that port. A number of signals being made and repeated round the Island, a copy of which Captain Rowley had by him, which came from some

of the prizes, and I was directed from the same not to get any more provisions on deck than what could be put into the boats when they returned from the *Leopard*. At noon that ship made signal for a strange sail S.W., and soon after we discovered a ship under jury topmast. The *Leopard's* signal was made to chase her. [As] the *Otter* was to windward coming down, her signal was made to proceed on and repeat signals

---

[1] This was the Walcheren Expedition, which sailed for the Scheldt on 28th July, 1809, the fleet commanded by Rear-Admiral Sir Richard Strachan and piloted, in effect, by the flag-captain, Sir Home Popham. All forces were withdrawn from Walcheren by the end of the year. The *Otter* brought news of the expedition sailing, not of its failure.

between the *Leopard* and us. At 3 the *Leopard* made the signal that the chase, a frigate, had anchord in Black River. We immediately bore up and made all sail to join her; we soon got within sight of her and found she was in the entrance of Black River inside a strong battery. A dark night coming on, we were obliged to relinquish all idea of attacking her, and we soon after haul'd off. Little wind all night. The *Otter*

worked up close along shore, but the *Leopard* and *Raisonable* did not steer. During the night and all the following day light airs from E.S.E., very clear fine weather. At daylight in the morning of the 2nd instant was discovered coming down from the S.E., steering for the north point of the Isle of France, for Port Louis, six sail, of which four appear'd to be

2nd instant the French Squadron returnd to Port Louis, viz:
La Bellone [44].
La Manche [38].
La Minerva [44].
La Victor [22].
 Indiamen:
Charlton [26].
United Kingdom [26].

frigates; the *Otter* was near them, but being chased by one of the enemy's ships, she shaped her course for us and the French Commodore recall'd the ship sent after her. Still becalmd, it was truly vexing to be in our situation, [with] two fine ships, two-deckers, not a sick man on board either ship, and the enemy's men divided in their prizes, and probably sickly after such a long cruise; together with our having been in that very cruising track off and on Port Louis for nearly two months, waiting for their return. How much they appear'd to have been favor'd, the *Venus* having come down to westward of the Island, drew us all from Port Louis, then becalm'd for two whole days in the presence of the French squadron and their prizes, and what was more vexing to me, as I was senior Lieut.[1], had we been fortunate enough to have been able to bring any of them to action, the major part of them would have fell into our pofsefsion; however it was not to be so, Providence had so directed it in favor of the enemy, and therefore we must be contented with whatever Divine Providence shall be pleased to dispense. Those ships of the enemy named above had been cruising in the Bay of

Bengal since September last. I mean the frigates *La Bellone*, *Manche*, and *Venus*—that ship that escaped into Black River on the 31st ult. The ships captured [included] the *Minerva*, a fine forty-gun frigate belonging to Portugal, only left Calcutta the preceding day of her capture by *La Bellone*, as

---

[1] A First Lieutenant would be promoted Commander almost automatically after a successful action. In this case he would have been given command of one of the captured frigates.

follows: That ship was cruising off the Sand Heads in quest of our trade. She was alone at this period, when the *Minerva* came out of the River Hoogley on her way to Europe, the French Frigate on her approaching hoisted English colours, and the Portuguese took her for an English ship, and made no preparation for action, tho' they must have known at Calcutta that the Bay of Bengal is seldom or never without one or more French frigates there, and it was necefsary to have been very cautious how they went near a ship of war without being completely ready for action. However, they was so certain of her being an English frigate that they bore up and ran to leeward and ahead of the *Bellone*, and when the *Minerva* was within musket shot the Frenchman gave him a full broadside, double shotted, which threw the Portuguese into the greatest consternation and confusion. In vain did the Captain entreat his officers and crew to defend their ship. A few—and very few—came to their quarters. Those fired most of the guns then loaded, and soon after, receiving two or three broadsides in a raking position, which killed or wounded those few brave fellows that had endeavoured to defend their ship with their brave Captain, finding that nothing could save the ship from the superiority of their, [i.e., the French], management and courage, the colours of the *Minerva* was hauld down and Commodore Du Perry said that he had arrived at the summit of his wishes in taking a frigate equally as large as his own; this was observed to some of the English Officers then prisoners on board *La Bellone*. Some of those officers observed to the Commodore that he must recollect that she was not an English Frigate, to which Du Perry replied, it's all the same, it was one of our Ally's. This ship was very fortunate for she soon after fell in with the *Victor*, a French privateer of eighteen guns, purchased by Government in India, and commanded by the Honble Edward Stopford; the *Bellone* came up with that sloop about 10 o'clock at night, and showed her lights all at once, hailing of the *Victor* to strike to His Imperial Majesty's frigate *La Bellone*. The *Victor* answered it with a broad side. She was hauld the second time by the *Bellone* to strike, but answered as before, the *Bellone* then opened a fire on her, fifteen 24-pounders on her main deck and ten 36-pound carronades on her quarter-deck and forecastle. The second broadside unrigged the little

The French Squadron return to Port Louis with their prizes.
La Bellone.
La Manche.
Ships of War prizes: *Minerva, Victor.*
India Ships prizes: *United Kingdom. Charlton.*

Victor, knock'd away her wheel and she became unmanageable. In this situation the *Bellone*, having ceased firing, hail'd her, to know if she had struck. They did not answer, but, firing a few guns at intervals, they now observed the Frenchman about to give them another broadside. Then Capt. Stopford call'd his officers round him and observed it was no use to hold out [in] an action of such great disparity of force on their side, and reluctantly directed the colours to be haul'd down, and hailed the *Bellone* that they had done so. The same cruise she took the *Charlton* and *United Kingdom*, Indiamen, all of them arrived safe with their prizes into Port Louis. The *Minerva* and *Victor* were both Commifsioned at sea by Commodore Du Perry, who had the Captain General's authority to do so, by every Ship of War that fell into their hands as prizes. They entered Port Louis at 11 o'clock, and salutes was fired by the *Bellone* and returned by Fort Imperial, and what was most mortifying to us was the sternmost ship had

Raisonable.
Leopard.
Otter
blockading them.

just entered that Port, before we got a breeze from the northward going eight knots, and by noon we were close in within reach of shells, and reconnoitred the port. We stood off and on Port Louis, expecting some more of their prizes would be coming down, and on the 3rd observed a ship coming down from S.E., supposed one of the prizes to the French squadron. As we were some way to leeward of the Port we made all sail in chase and as she found that she could not effect getting round Cannonaire Point for our Squadron, she soon ran on shore near Grand Bay and Cannonaire Battery.

1810.
3rd January.

It was judged by Commodore Rowley practicable to destroy her. Accordingly, boats was prepared and signals made to the *Leopard* and *Otter* to be ready with their boats at 9 p.m. Being Senior Lieutenant, I volunteered the command of this most daring enterprise. This vefsel had anchor'd between two batteries on Cannonaire Point, within a musket shot of the principal one, of six 36-pounders. The Squadron kept near the Point and the enemy appear'd perfectly aware of our intention as we observed about two hundred men, soldiers, marching towards that post at sunset, so that we expected a warm undertaking. At 8 o'clock the boats of the *Leopard* and *Otter* came alongside the *Raisonable* where everything was arranged in order. To complete this expedition two boats were to have combustibles in and to act as fireboats. The

93

whole number of boats was eight, two barges, and [the others?] not large cutters and pinnaces. Two other boats were to cut the cable, and four should board on the bow or quarter as circumstances should appear most expedient when we got near her. Watch words were appointed for every movement, whether to advance, re-inforce or retreat, &c., &c. This was the plan agreed on by myself and the officers appointed for this service. At 9 o'clock we left the *Raisonable* then about three miles to the N.W. of Cannonaire Point, we pull'd from that time till 2 a.m. and there appeared such a strong lee current with fresh S.E. wind that it retarded our progrefs greatly, some of the boats pulling very bad; so much so, that I frequently, in the *Raisonable's* Barge, lost sight of the boats in the rear. And I am under the imprefsion (from some unknown circumstance) that several of the boats appear'd not to exert themeslves so much as might have been expected, not but it might be all for the best, for really I think had all the boats pull'd as well as the one I was in we should have reach'd the place of destination long ere midnight. But really in doing so I am of opinion from the darknefs of the night, together with our very imperfect knowledge of her situation, that it would have been ten to one against our completing the object in view. However, I did wish that we could have reach'd the spot, but so Providence appeard to direct us that we should not arrive at it, a very strong current having prevail'd that night, going more than two knots per hour, that at twilight I observed that if anything we were further from the place where the ship was on shore, having drifted away to the N.E. of it. I then, with the concurrence of Lieut. Dwyer, send the mates of the *Leopard* and *Otter* and *Raisonable*, the only boats in the van (the rear boats were almost out of sight) to leeward and astern, and daylight coming on, together with the impofsibility of making the place of attack, I ordered the boats to step their masts and run down to and take the worst sailing boats in tow. I bore up in the barge and went to leeward of the whole and took the *Otter's* cutter in tow, which was not provided with a sail. I desired Lieut. Dwyer, Junior of the *Raisonable*, to inform the Commodore of the circumstance which had led to the failure, as well as why I went after this boat so far to leeward. I was however happy to find that we got on board and hoisted in all

An Indiaman prize to the French Squadron, having ran inshore near Cannonaire Point to prevent her being taken by the English Squadron, an attempt made to destroy her by the boats failed owing to a strong current set the boats in an opposite direction.

N.B.—Had we succeeded in all probability we should have been sacrificed to the impetuous French soldiery, whom we saw marching in strong bodies to protect the vefsel on shore.

4th instant at noon
this day was detach'd
to go to windward
of the Island
Leopard.
Otter.

the boats before daylight, so that the enemy would not know that we had made the attempt during the night. The Commodore received me with his usual mildnefs and said, " Well, Walters, you could not get to the ship owing to the strong current setting to the N.E. ? " I replied that was the reason together with some of the boats pulling very heavy—not but I had an opinion still left relative to it. However, I shall end the narrative, and being a good deal fatigued as well as disappointed, I went to bed to get a little rest, it being 4 o'clock. At 6 a sail was discovered off Cape Brabant, bore up in chase of her and made all sail, *Leopard* and *Otter* in company. It proved to be the *Boadicea*, very sickly, having caught the contagion from some French prisoners taken in the *Young*

At 10 p.m. *Boadicea*
parted company for
the Cape of Good
Hope.

Eliza prize, brig. This was a great disappointment to us, as we were going to deliver to her all the surplus provisions, and expected to have proceeded to the Cape that evening. However, when the Captain of the *Boadicea* came on board, he informed the Commodore that they had about thirty people in their hammocks, in a very bad fever. In consequence of the same we met a reverse; for in lieu of delivering our surplus provisions, we had to receive the *Boadicea's*. At 10 p.m. the *Boadicea* and *Creole* Schooner parted company, and the *Raisonable*

made all pofsible sail, turning to windward to join His Majesty's Ships *Leopard* and *Otter*, cruising to the East of the Isle of France. On the 6th instant we had a very dark dismal night with heavy squalls of rain, accompanied with thunder and lightning. In the morning we fell in with the above ships and joined company with them, and commenced cruising together, at the distance of twenty leagues from any part of the Island. After daylight we extended our distance from each other so as just to be able to repeat signals from one ship to the other, by which judicious arrangement the ships

Raisonable
Leopard
Otter
  cruising to wind'd of
the Isle of France.

covered ground enough to observe what vefsels may be bound to the Isle of France, let them make for either port in that Island. The *Leopard* [was] to the Northward, *Raisonable* to Southward, and the *Otter* in the centre. Captain Rowley, who had been many years upon this station in the preceding War, by which he was acquainted with every thing relative to the situation of the enemy's squadron, was aware that as the Americans judged that the English blockading squadron would in all probability return to the Cape ere this period, that they would be flocking to the markets with such supplies as would answer for provision in the completing the enemy's ships for their ensuing cruise in the Spring, this being considered the hurricane months. And the French [would] endeavour to keep all their vefsels safe in port during this period, knowing that the speculative merchants of the United States would try the hazard of the voyage, being aware of its being a very lucrative thing should they steer clear of the English Squadron. Nor was the Captain out in his conjecture. Having cruised for several days as described above, having extreme fine weather, at 7 a.m. the morning of 10th instant, we discovered a brig having all sail set, coming down from the S.E. steering about N.W. for the N.E. end of Isle de France. We gave chase to her, and on bringing her to, she hoisted American Colours, and proved to be the *Charles*, an American Brig from Rio Janeiro, laden with sundry articles of provisions, wet and dry, and a quantity of wine. The supercargo on his coming on board informed us that he was bound to Bombay, and that he took the land that he was steering for to be Roderigue, where, he said, being in want of a supply of water, he was going to replenish his stock. They had no invoice of her cargo, no clearance from Customs House, without a log book, and no account of her reckoning, consequently there was nothing to obstruct her being a lawful prize, although the Master and Supercargo persisted in it that they were certain she would be liberated. Sent a mate and ten men to navigate her to the Cape of Good Hope. Very pleasant agreeable weather.

On the 17th instant joined company His Majesty's Ship *Magicienne* [36], arrived from England, last from Cape of Good Hope, to re-inforce the Squadron, which ship had recaptured the Honble Company's ship *Windham*[1], outward bound with a cargo of Military stores, and had sent her to the Cape of Good Hope. She had been captured by *Venus* and *Manche*, French Frigates, on her pafsage to India, after a chase of three days, when the latter ship came up with [her,] and a spirited action commenced. The *Windham* had about three hundred troops on board, which were distributed at

Marginal notes:

Captured the *Charles*, American Brig laden with provision and wine, bound to Port Louis.

Long. Roderigue 68° 00′ E.
Long. I. de France 58° 30′ E.
Out in his reckoning 9°30′

17th instant joined *Magicienne*.

Account of the capture of the *Windham* by the French Frigates *La Venus* and *Manche*.

[1] The ship which Walters himself was later to command, as Agent Afloat, in 1813. She was on her fifth voyage when captured and, after her period as a transport, did one more voyage (to China) in 1816-17.

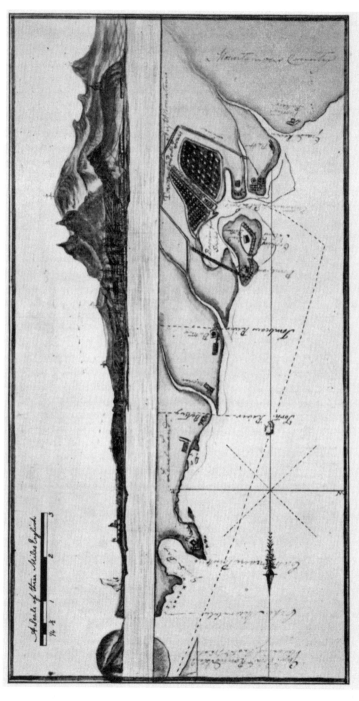

PLATE 9.—Port Louis, Mauritius or Ile de France. Reproduced from a sketch map and water-colour, the work of Lieutenant Walters.

PLATE 10.—Sketch of H.M. Ship *Courageux* (Commodore Wilkinson) proceeding from the Baltic fleet to reinforce the Squadron on the North American Station, 1812. Reproduced from a water-colour by Lieutenant Walters.

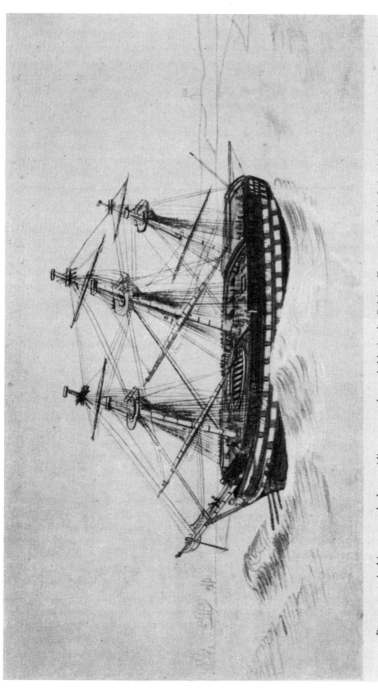

PLATE II.—A ship unnamed, shown riding out a gale, probably in the Baltic. From an unfinished sketch by Lieutenant Walters.

PLATE 12—Relics of Lieutenant Walters, now in the possession of Mr. Frank Walters Mills;

her quarters at the great guns, except about one hundred at small arms. Such a reception they gave the *Manche*, that in about twenty minutes she sheèred off nor did that ship attempt to come alongside her until the *Venus* came up, which was some time after, she being a dull sailer. The *Windham*, having most of her running rigging shot away prevented her avoiding an action with the second frigate, being much larger and mounting fifty guns. Notwithstanding, Captain Stewart in the most gallant manner resisted this superior force, and did not strike until the ship was unmanageable, by his sails and rigging being cut to pieces, and the *Manche* keeping astern of her, raking of her, which swept away great numbers of her crew and soldiers. But at length they were compel'd to strike after a most gallant defence. We soon after discovered a vefsel which proved [to be] the *Dispatch* Schooner, which was constantly employed in keeping up the communication between the Captain General of the French Forces residing at Port Louis and the General in the Command of the Isle De Bonaparte, commonly call'd the Isle of Bourbon. After the *Magicienne* joined us we all bore up and ran to leeward off Port Louis. As Commodore Rowley was about to proceed for the Cape, our ship being almost out of provision and stores, having been out eight months, this schooner before mentioned [was sighted]. She had been chased by all the ships of the squadron separately between those Islands, but never one could get near her owing to her superior management, for she seldom left any port until dusk, and when any of our ships pursued her she ran as long as they could discern her under sail, but the moment it became dark they down with her masts, which was upon the principle of the joint of a carpenter's rule. The whole of us joined in the chase as per margin. The third ship, *Magicienne*, which sail'd very superior to the rest of the ships, being just out from port, well down in the water, being complete in every article of stores and provisions for six months, which enabled her to get close to her. The moon having favor'd us until midnight. That ship fired upwards of 50 times at her with her chase guns, altho' she was close under her bows; notwithstanding, they could not hit her. Once I experienced a similar firing in chase.[1] Through the smallnefs of the object and a great sea she escaped unhurt,

[1] This was when he was in the *Argo*. See page 17.

and we lost sight of her the moment the moon went below the horizen. The Squadron having chased this vefsel off the land a long way, as soon as we mifsed her, the Commodore tack'd, as did the Squadron and stood in for Port Louis, and at daylight we observ'd the French Schooner which we had been in chase of, about six miles to windward of the van ship the *Magicienne*, which ship had every sail set in chase of her. Having a light wind together with her sweeps, she went two feet to the Frigate's one, but she was a considerable way off that Island. Soon after 8 a.m. we discovered three sail, two off Port Louis, one off Round Island. The Schooner got in to Grand Bay safe. We made all sail to find out what ships they were, which proved to be, soon after, per signal, His Majesty's Ships *Sirius* [36], *Iphigenia* [36], and *Sapphire*, returnd from their cruise off Seychells in quest of those ships which got safe into Port Louis. On the 2nd instant the whole of their Captains dined with the Commodore, and at 8 p.m. we parted Company with the Squadron, then under the command of Captain Pym of the *Sirius*. We proceeded for the Cape of Good Hope. It was understood that Captain Lambert of the *Iphigenia* would be the senior officer of the Squadron, as Capt. Pym in the *Sirius* was to proceed for Madagascar to procure water, if pofsible, and other supplies. We had fine weather, and was likely to make a quick pafsage. About six days after we were overtaken by that ship owing to her not being able to approach that Coast having bad weather, being the rainy season. Captain Rowley desired him to make the best of his way to the Cape. The *Otter* soon after joined company and remain'd with us. We had fine weather until we made Lagullus Cape, when we experienced very heavy S.W. gale which lasted for four days, and such was the current sailing, that although we were laying to under our storm staysails with a very heavy sea occasioned by an amazing strong westerly current, that set us to windward three knots per hour, and when it became moderate the fifth day we were abreast of the Hanglip or False Cape. Then the wind shifted to the eastward which enabled us to set studding sails, and the following day we anchor'd in Table Bay after a cruise of eight months.

During the last violent gale off Cape Lagullas the lashing of the Commodore's dining table gave way when at dinner,

18th instant.
Joined company
Sirius
Magicienne
Sapphire
off Port Louis.

10th February, 1810.
Raisonable returns from a cruise of eight months.
Table Bay.

February, 1810.

by which the worthy man broke his arm, and several of the gentlemen his guests received some heavy blows, falling against the guns in the sudden lurch she took. I am now arrived at that part of my manuscript relative to my views being in the most favourable way for promotion. We were all acquainted that those Islands were to be attack'd on the arrival of the troops from India, as also that Captain Rowley would have the chief command of the Naval arrangements, and of course would have a chance of recommending such of his officers as he conceived had a claim by the reduction of Saint Paul's. I became Senior Lieutenant of the *Raisonable*, under his command; the former First Lieut. having been sent home with the Dispatches of that place having been attack'd, and the works of the Batteries demolished, guns renderd uselefs by bursting them and knocking their trunnions off, all the shipping and public stores captured and brought away. Those Dispatches to the Admiralty, Commodore Rowley considered would be the means of getting Lieut. Bluett promoted to the rank of a Commander. He also went prize master of *La Caroline*, frigate, our prize, which he was to quit on his arrival at the Cape, and to proceed with the Dispatches for England in another prize, the *Grappler*, Brig. Under the imprefsion that Bluett was now provided for, that I should stand the next on the list for a step, more particularly as Captain R. had been very propitious to me of late, I was almost certain of being in a fair channel to facilitate my preferment. This appear'd more conspicuous to me for during our pafsage into the Cape he was pointing out what he wish'd done to the ship, afsuring me that we should not be long in port, and recommended every exertion to be used in equipping the ship in her sails and rigging, and all pofsible expedition in getting on board the provisions, water, and stores. I need scarce observe that I afsured him it should be duly attended to, with the most prompt obedience and alacrity. But how soon was my views reversed, such is the fate of human caprice, that on our arrival [we] found that Lieut. Bluett was still at the Cape and not gone to England with the Dispatches. The Admiral,[2] not considering the Dispatches of that consequence to send an officer home with them, had sent them by a Military pafsenger in one of the Indiamen. This brought

[2] Vice-Admiral William O'Brien Drury.

99

me second Lieutenant again. And, in the run of one week, some orders having arrived from England, by which the *Raisonable* was ordered home immediately, and to take charge of the convoy in Table Bay; the *Leopard* being also ordered home. It appear'd, as that ship was the Admiral's Flagship, that the Admiralty had directed him to hoist it on board any ship he might make choice of, and, as they had done so, he considered that by the same rule he might take which Captain he pleased to command the ship. Accordingly it was arranged by the Commander-in-Chief that the *Boadicea* should be his flagship, and that Captain Rowley should command her, and that Captain Hatley of that ship should command the *Raisonable*. The officers of the *Boadicea* were distributed three to the *Raisonable* and one to the *Otter*. The *Boadicea's* Lieutenants were appointed by the Admiral, being his followers, and most of them had been acting-Commanders, but superceded, so that when Captain Rowley took leave of us he was pleased to observe that it was with regret he could not take any of his officers with him into the *Boadicea*, as the Admiral had arranged all that, but he said if he could be of any service in future, in obtaining ships for us, &c., he should be very happy. We all exprefsed our disappointment in not having the pleasure of going out under his command in the *Raisonable*, and in being parted after being with him nearly five years. Capt. Hatley[1] took the command of the *Raisonable* and soon after we sail'd from Table Bay in company with H.M. Sloops, *Charwell* and *Caledon* and four Indiamen. After a pleasant pafsage, though a very long one owing to some of the Indiamen sailing very ill (we found it necefsary to carry very little sail to keep company with the convoy) we arrived at Chapel Valley Bay, Island of St. Helena, and found at this anchorage His Majesty's Ship *Argo*,[2] and the *Ocean*, East Indiaman, laden with sundry stores for the use of the Island. Here we remained until the arrival of His Majesty's Ship *Inconstant*, which ship being Senior Officer took the command of the Squadron, and convoy. She had just arrived from England, last from Table Bay, having been on shore on some small rocky Islands abreast of Saldanna Bay, and was very near lost. She was damaged so much that she was obliged to

March.
Captain Rowley appointed to the *Boadicea*.
Captain Hatley appointed to the *Raisonable*.

Raisonable, *Charwell* and *Caledon* sailed from Table Bay with a convoy for England.
April, 1810.
1st Inst.

Inconstant. [36]
Argo. [44]
Raisonable. [64]
Caledon.
Charwell. } [Sloops]
Indiamen:
  Streatham
  Devaynes
  Ocean
  Tottenham
  and three whalers.

---

[1] On whose efficiency the author had his views. See above, page 86.
[2] His own first ship, though he does not comment on the fact.

be hove down immediately on her arrival, all her main keel was gone close to the rabbets for the garboard strake, her cutwater gone close to the dead wood, and her heel in a similar state. Mr. John Clarke, the master shipwright of the Naval Yard at the Cape of Good Hope, being a clever man in his profefsion, patchd her up so complete with sheet lead, hides, tallow, oakum, and pitch, that it was deemed safe for her to return to England. As the Spring would be coming on, and having no materials to give her such a repair as she stood in need of, it was judged expedient to send her home with all pofsible despatch, and the *Raisonable* was directed in case of blowing weather to keep close to that frigate during our pafsage. We did not leave this delightful place until 1st May, having been very comfortable, dining and visiting the Governor and the principal officers and merchants of the Garrison and Town. We left the *Argo* at that anchorage to take home the next convoy expected there. We had very fine weather all the pafsage; [and] the *Raisonable* had one of the bad sailing whalers in tow. Remarkable pleasant weather, and nothing occurred of any consequence in the Squadron and convoy. It was somewhat singular how very superior the *Inconstant* sail'd to any ship of the Squadron. I seldom remember her to have anything set but double reef'd topsails, and very rarely would set his foresail after speaking a ship. On the 12th instant, we crofsed the Equator in Longitude 22° 50′ west, and without seeing any ship or vefsel until we arrived in the mouth of the Channel. Soon after we made St. Agnes's light on Scilly, and easterly wind prevailing soon after retarded our progrefs for three days. When it became fair we crowded all sail for the Downs. Abreast of the Dunnose we parted company with the *Inconstant*, *Caledon*, and *Charwell* for Spithead, and the following evening anchor'd in the Downs. Found the North Sea Fleet here under the command of Vice-Admiral Sir Edward Pellew, Bt., who came on board the *Raisonable* immediately we anchord, to see Captain Rowley, who he expected was in her; but finding that he was not there, he put off in great haste and went to sea that evening. Following day we weighed, and proceeded for the Nore. Owing to light baffling winds, we did not reach that anchorage til Sunday, 9th, and the same day we got a pilot and went up the Medway and anchor'd in

May, 1810.
Sail'd from Saint Helena with above ships exceptg *Argo*.

June.

1st July, 1810. Made St. Agnes Light. Scilly.

4th instant the ships [of] war parted co. for Spithead.
5th instant anchord in the Downs.

9th instant anchord at the Nore.

long reach. In the evening moor'd ship, came alongside the Hoys and lighters for the guns and stores. Commenced clearing ship. Next day parties of seamen were sent off, fifty men in each, to several ships fitting out as troopships with all pofsible dispatch. I was sent with one to the *Diadem* and superintended her equipment, and afsisted in taking her out to the Nore. When we returnd to our ship again (this was on the 27th of July) we found the *Raisonable* all ready to be paid off, all her stores and everything return'd to the yard,

Raisonable paid off at Chatham. 31st July, 1810.

the ship haul'd alongside a hulk, and on the morning of the 31st July we landed the ship's company by divisions at the Dockyard, where they received a certain part of their pay. Some of whom had seven years' pay due to them, and most of them five. They were allowed a fortnight's leave and on their return were to be paid their residue of pay. Here ends the *Raisonable's* Narrative.

1810. August 31st.

Chatham: Having superintended the people in their payments, Captain Hatley and the Lieutenants and officers of the Ward Room, and gentlemen of the cockpit dined together, which in general is customary previous to our parting, and very jovial we were till midnight, when we separated and each went to their respective lodgings, quite happy and

August 1st.

exhilarated. The following day, that fine new built ship the *Impregnable* was launched from the King's yard; the whole of the *Raisonable's* officers remained to witnefs this most magnificent sight, which took place at quarter past meridian, [she] having hung, after the spar shore had been knocked away, near twenty minutes, occasioned by the forefoot of the ship having rested on the upper block, which had not been observed by any of the artificers until full ten minutes after everything was removed for her going off. However, in five minutes some smart young shipwrights extricated her, and away she went in a most majestic state, which was greeted by acclamations of the surrounding multitude of spectators of the first distinction, and a most beautiful sight it was. She is a second-rate of ninety-eight guns.

I had received letters from my parents informing me that my poor Mother was much better in health than she had been for several years, and who entreated that I would make all possible despatch to visit her, having been only one week home on leave since my entering into His Majesty's Service in the year 1798; an elapse of twelve years. I must own I had a great wish to see my worthy old parents, who always testified their high esteem and affection for me, and I was about to prepare to pay them a visit. My brother also paid me a visit during the time I remained in London, and, the poor fellow, I was very glad to see him and [he] testified his affection in return. I left London the 4th instant (on my way down to Devonshire) in the morning at 4 o'clock, and supped at the White Hart Inn in Salisbury. Slept there that night, and the following day hired a post chaise and went out to the village of Fordingbridge, where my old friend and mefsmate, Reverend David Griffiths, served as curate to that and another parish in Hants. I remained with him four days. He was married and had one child, appear'd very comfortable. I was received with every mark of friendship, and received a most hearty welcome. I should have stayed double that time, but for my Mother's wish to see me. On the afternoon of the 8th instant I took leave of Mrs. Griffiths and little one, and was accompanied into Salisbury by Doctr. Griffiths and another old shipmate, a Mr. Maley, midshipman, and we dined together at the White Hart Inn, and I took leave of them at 5 o'clock and set off for Exeter, and travelled all night, and the next day at Noon we arrived and put up at the London Inn, Exeter. Stopt there that night, and the next morning went off by the Fly Coach, a stage that runs to and from Plymouth, where we reach'd the same evening, having dined on the road

August 12th.

at Ivy Bridge. I put up at a respectable tavern, and got myself shifted and dined there. After a comfortable repast I went to pay my poor dear Mother a visit in the vicinity of Stonehouse. On my arrival at her residence, I knocked at the door, which was opened by [my] youngest sister, who appear'd to be much affected at [my] arrival, having been absent upwards of seven years. On my entering my Mother's apartment, the poor old lady could not speak to me, being quite choked with tears, and heavy at heart, till at length, being relieved by the deluge of tears, she became a little composed, and after the first greeting was over, and reason resumed her quiet again, then did I enjoy the conversation of a most affectionate, tender Mother, a happinefs that did

Devonshire.

not often fall to my lot.

Samuel Walters' homecoming raises a number of problems. To begin with, his brother, Miles, had left the sea and gone to work, "poor fellow", in London. The suggestion of pity may relate to the circumstances, whatever they were, which occasioned Miles' retirement from the Navy; if, indeed, he had ever been in it. Samuel, in any case, was the more successful of the two, a commissioned officer and one who had not done too badly in prize-money; a man who could afford a post-chaise when he wanted one; a man who might rise in the service as others who had served in the *Raisonable* had done. Of Miles all too little is known. He is said to have been married at St. Sepulchre's Church, Shoreditch. He was the father of at least three sons and one daughter, one of the sons (born the next year, 1st November, 1811) being named Samuel after his uncle. Unfortunately for subsequent genealogists, he was born of dissenting parents in a coasting vessel somewhere between Bideford and London. The Devonshire connection was evidently being maintained. As for occupation, it is clear that Miles, beginning as shipwright and carpenter, had become a maker and gilder of picture frames; perhaps with some skill in retouching old or damaged canvases. If this is the fact, it would account for his doing a little painting on his own, as he seems to have done. To the subsequent career of Miles' son, the younger Samuel, we shall have occasion to return.

Lieutenant Walters found his parents—or at any rate his mother—at Stonehouse, Plymouth. It is not clear in what year they had migrated there, but Henrietta, the sister who was there to greet him, was already married to a Plymouth man in 1809. Her husband was Captain John Rodd, a merchant seaman, and the marriage took place at Stoke Damerel—the parish church of Plymouth Dock—on the 4th December in that year. The clue to this migration seems to lie in the family tradition that John Walters, the father, was clerk of works at Dartmoor and helped prepare the plans of both the prison and the church. For this tradition there is some evidence, as we shall see, and it fits in with the early history of that penal establishment. It was intended for prisoners of war, which were becoming, after 1803, something of a problem. Many were kept at that time in six hulks moored in Hamoaze, Plymouth Harbour; others being in Mill Prison and still more at Portsmouth. The hulks were good from a security point of view but had become something of a scandal. This must be admitted even if we believe only a tenth of what the author of "*Mes Pontons*" has to say about them. The hulks belonged to the Transport Board and it was an official of that Admiralty branch who reported favourably (July 20th, 1805) on the project for building an alternative shore establishment at Tor Royal on Dartmoor. The site, then empty moorland, belonged to the Duchy of Cornwall and its use for this purpose owed much to the initiative of Thomas Tyrwhit, Esq., Lord Warden of the Stannaries and Secretary to the Prince Regent. The foundation stone was laid by him on March 20th, 1806, and the contractors (Messrs. Isbell, Rowe and Co.) went busily ahead on a plan drawn by the architect, Mr. Daniel Alexander. The scheme was on a large scale, the buildings being designed to accommodate 5,000-7,000 prisoners under a guard of 300-500 troops. The cost amounted to £66,815, the spending of which added something to the prosperity of Plymouth, which gratefully elected Mr. Tyrwhit its M.P. for 1806-1812. The prisoners (5,000 of them) were marched up-country from the hulks in May-June, 1809, and the Transport Agent, Captain Isaac Cotgrave, R.N., went with them to his new " ship." There were at that time no other buildings at Princetown (as it is now called) except the Inn, which is still there, and a few cottages. The village mostly grew up during the next few years, the Parish Church being built between 1810 and 1815 with French prisoners to do the masonry and Americans the woodwork. From all this it seems probable that John Walters was given some sort of overseer's employment, presumably in 1806 or between then and 1809. As the village did not yet exist he would naturally leave his wife in Plymouth until accommodation could be built. This, no doubt, is what he did, which would account for his absence when Samuel visited Plymouth in 1810 That he supervised the work on the church is likely enough. It may be relevant to remind ourselves that Captain James Bowen (of Ilfracombe) was one of the Commissioners of the Transport Board in 1803-1806 and did not necessarily lose his influence there even after his temporary return to sea as Captain of the Fleet under Lord St. Vincent.

Samuel Walters was ashore, presumably at Plymouth and Dartmoor, until November, 1810, when he was appointed, as we shall see, third Lieutenant of the *Courageux* [74]. This had the effect of bringing him back to Plymouth with great opportunities for leave while the ship was in dock after her grounding on the Skerries. It is from this period that dates the first evidence of his interest in art. It is a miniature portrait of himself, painted on ivory and reproduced as the frontispiece of this book. It shows him smartly dressed in the uniform of the period, and looking much less than his 32 years. Round-faced, with a good mouth and chin, sensitive nostrils and large dark eyes, he looks a thoughtful man; perhaps a little uncertain of himself; hardly ruthless enough, maybe, for success in his chosen trade. It may, incidentally, be a self-portrait; the proof, in that case, of having practised painting for some considerable time. On the reverse side an inscription reads:

Samuel Walters, son of J. & Mary Walters of the Parish Ilfracombe in the County Devonshire, baptised 10th June, 1778 and at sea on the *Ocean* 1796-1798. Entered the Navy as (Midshipman) Lieut. 8th March, 1805, presented this to his Mother at Stonehouse in March, 1811, to perpetuate his memory and as a token of sincere affection and esteem.

From this same period dates the purchase of some religious tracts, apparently bought by Samuel for his mother to read and later pasted by him in a manuscript book bound by Vicary and Co., 15, Market Street, Plymouth Dock. He draws attention to particular items—" a Hymn worth reading," &c.—and writes " Good " in the margin of " Contemplations in a Church-yard," opposite a favourite passage. On the first page of *The Christian Guardian* for January, 1810, he recommends certain items and adds " Mary Walters, resides at Stonehouse—well afsured she delights in these books." He evidently recovered this volume after his mother's death. From his sister, who inherited it, this has descended, with other relics, to Mr. Frank Walters Mills, of Pointe Claire, near Montreal.

There now follows Samuel's account of his time in the *Courageux*, beginning with the mishap which cut short her first voyage and ending with her escape from shipwreck on the South-West Anholt Reef in 1812.

> *Memo.*
> Appointed Lieutenant of His Majesty's Ship *Courageux* [74], 24th November, 1810. Joined her at Spithead, 2nd December. Commd. Captain Philip Wilkinson. She was then fitting for sea. In January, 1811, working down Channel, dark thick night with rain, wind W.S.W. 21st a.m., little before daylight standing out from Torbay or Brixham Point, ran on the Skerries 5 or 6 miles E. by N. of the Start, and remained there nearly 3 hours, but came off without sustaining any material damage. Made but little water. However, she was docked at Plymouth and the Captain and Master reprimanded by sentence of a Court Martial which was ordered. The Master was a clever man. Captain said to be in the sick list, but who did not leave the guidance of the ship to the Master, but strongly urged that the ship should be kept working down as close to the English coast as possible, in order it's presumed to put into Plymouth on her passage to Basque Roads, which he succeeded in completely, and remained upwards of three months in Hamoaze, when she was ordered to join the Baltic Fleet.

This happened solely by the Captain's cunning,
The Master's advice invariably shunning,
A clever man in every branch of his profefsion,
If the Captain only to him would listen.

But when it came to be discufs'd in Court
The Captain fain would be in the sick report,
Leaving the blame of this misapt and time
On the Master's shoulders he was inclined.

But scrutiny soon unfold'd the matter fair,
That the Captain dictated, nay would not hear
The Master exprefsd his great dislike
Keeping the coast so close aboard, by night.

But when the mischief was past, and all over, he,
The Captain, wished the whole should be
The Master's error in running the ship aground,
But proof came out, and it was found

That if the Captain had allowed him to follow right
His own good judgment in the night,
Would have prevented her going on shore
And neither would [have] been perplexed any more.

This good Master was soon appointed to the *Ocean* [98], of a second rate, by a former Captain's application. A worthy man his succefsor, very fair but very obstinate and contumacious. The ship joined the Baltic Fleet and after remaining till the Autumn, 1811, returnd to England with convoy. In December of this year, *St. George* [98] (Flag Ship of worthy Rear-Admiral Reynolds) with *Defence* [74], ships of the line, and *Fanny* Brig, were wrecked on the coast of Jutland. The following year we became Senior Officer in the great Belt, and in November we were, with the *Plantaganet* [74], ordered to England to be sent on the Coast of America, being in resemblance, it was thought, at a distance of Frigates, having no poops.

[sidenote:] Appointed to the *Courageux* per commifsion dated 24th November, 1810; joined 2nd December, Spithead. On going down Channel to join the Squadron in Basque Roads, got on shore on the Skerries, near Start a.m. 21st January, 1811. Docked 3 months in Hamoaze, ordered to Baltic. Near danger coming home—gale and large convoy. Next summer also attach'd Baltic Fleet. 12th Nov. ordered to England. In night of 13 got on shore, on the S.W. Anholt reef. Very near being lost. Remained on the reef near three hours. Came off with the lofs of her rudder.

The Following Lines is relative to the Courageux *getting on shore on the S.W. Anholt Reef on the night of 13th November, 1812.*

In Autumn it was of the twelfth year,
The eleventh month it is very clear,
Ere midnight of the thirteenth day,
A fine British Bark was near cast away.

It was the second Summer she was on the station,
In the Baltic Sea it was adjacent;
An American War having commenced
This gallant ship was to proceed hence.

But headstrong power none could prevent,
As it was determined by pilot's consent
That the ship should proceed from Zealand shore
Tho' the darkest night prevailing o'er.

Amid the numerous Rocks and sand,
Down the Cattegat the ship did stand;
The wind was fresh from the South West,
And the Anholt light would be seen, the Master guefs'd.

But sad to record, ere the eleventh hour,
This majestic ship was plump on shore,
Under double reef'd topsails and fore course was she
Going eight knots under Anholt's lee.

Dismal was this, many did despair
That her dissolution was very near;
She thumped heavy, and masts did play
That in their obedience to the prow, would jump away.

Awful the grinding noise of keel and heel
With an unusual motion made the crew to reel,
The rudder being most oppressed and bound
But soon it got released and went to the ground.

Sail first being set to prefs her over the reef,
But striking harder without relief
Twas instantly clewed up and fast'd again anew
With willingnefs and zeal by her gallant crew.

108

At last the deleterious order to prepare
To throw the cannon over board. Oh what despair !
The Officer of the third post ventured to state,
Oh noble Chieftain pray hesitate !

Remember Sire, said this self same third,
With due submission, Pray let me be heard,
You own experiences of its baleful effects
As often tried and as often made wrecks.

Guns lying together on the sand equal to Rocks annoy
The bottom of the Bark, they may soon destroy;
And now it's blowing a gale of wind, what hopes
Impossible to save our lives could we get out the boats.

Stand Fast, the bold Commander said, Tis true
The wind is shifted for us. Set topsails anew
Square sails set and braced all aback. See hence
The wonderful care of Almighty's Providence.

The damage sustained by the *Courageux* on the reef was enough to
prevent her sailing, as planned, for the American station. She was evidently
paid off in March, 1813, leaving Walters to find another ship. One thing
apparent is that he had lost any chance of immediate promotion. It must
be understood, in this connection, that the step from Lieutenant to
Commander, like that from Commander to Captain, had little to do with
seniority. It could be gained by the recommendation of an Admiral, by
strong political interest ashore or by merit repeatedly shown in action.
For the officer without any particular interest, ashore or afloat, the chances
of promotion dwindled to one—the luck of being First Lieutenant in a
successful engagement. A battle, for this purpose, would do very well;
but a single ship action would do even better. After the capture, say, of
an enemy ship of sufficiently equal weight, the fortunate captain would
write a terse and modest report, usually concluding with a tribute to his
first lieutenant and other officers. " It gives me great pleasure to
remark to you, Sir," he would write " the zeal and gallantry of Lieutenant
Capstan, who led the boarding party." On receiving this, the Admiral
would enclose it in a letter to William Marsden, Esq., Secretary to their
Lordships; a letter which would say about the captain all that he had
nobly refrained from saying about himself. " The exertion " he would
conclude " of Captain Mainbrace and of Lieutenant Capstan, since they

have been upon the station, has excited my highest approbation." What would result from all this ? Little enough as far as the captain was concerned, unless the deed should have justified a knighthood. But the first lieutenant could almost count on promotion. "Lieutenant Capstan" he would expect to read in the gazette, "is promoted to the rank of Commander and appointed to the *Bulldog*." Apart, however, from the luck of an action, a first lieutenant could hardly expect promotion merely by being useful. That would tend merely to make him indispensable as first lieutenant and keep him in that office until he retired.

For Samuel Walters, then, all chance of promotion hinged on becoming a first lieutenant and so remaining until an action should bring him favourable notice in the gazette. His best chances had come when he was 2nd lieutenant in the *Raisonable*. First, Captain Corbet had offered him the vacancy of first lieutenant in the *Nereide;* an offer which Walters (see page 71) refused. His motives in refusing are understandable. He knew Corbet from the time (see page 64) when that officer had been in temporary command of the *Raisonable*, and he speaks of him elsewhere with respect— "That active and zealous officer, Captain Corbet" (page 77); "the celerity peculiar to the gallant Captn Corbet" (page 79)—but he probably detested the methods by which Corbet maintained discipline. At the same time, it was an opportunity missed. His next chance came with the promotion of Lieutenant Bluett, which actually made him, for the time being, the senior lieutenant of the *Raisonable*. This ended, however, in a disappointment which he clearly describes and which brought him back to England under a new captain and without much likelihood of Captain Rowley doing anything to forward his claims. When appointed to the *Courageux* he was third lieutenant under a captain he evidently disliked, and so probably remained until March, 1813. His chances of promotion had vanished.

His answer to the immediate problem was evidently to turn once more to Captain James Bowen, back at the Transport Board after organising the evacuation of the troops from Corunna in 1809. And Bowen, presumably offered him the only sort of vacancy he had in his gift—an appointment as Transport Agent. It was a post with certain attractions, carrying with it the virtual command of a ship, with naval pay and allowances. But acceptance of such a post meant abandoning hope of glory or promotion. Hired merchantmen taken up by the Transport Board were intended (mainly) to carry troops or stores from one place to another. The system was to leave the ship her own Master and Mates but put in, over their heads, an Agent Afloat who was to be obeyed "in the strictest Manner." Transports with such an Agent (always a naval lieutenant) were distinguished by a blue ensign and a " plain blue common pendant " and could exercise an authority by signal over such smaller transports as carried no Agent. A number of transports might sail in convoy, in which case one of them would carry a Principal Agent (Captain or Commander, R.N.) with a " Blue Broad Pendant " at the main-topmast-head, whose signals (failing naval escort) the rest would obey. In " Armed Transports "—not merely transports that were armed, as they mostly were—the Agent was termed Commander and was supported by Purser, Boatswain, Gunner, and Carpenter, all appointed by warrant and on naval pay. Walters was offered such an Armed Transport; and he accepted it. Some thirty-seven other Lieutenants had, at one time or another, done the same. They appeared separately in the List of Sea Officers. They were no longer, in the full sense, fighting men.

The ship to which Walters was appointed was none other than the *Windham*, East Indiaman, of 878 tons and 22 guns, managed by Mr. Andrews with Mr. William Blythe as Master. He would have heard all about the *Windham*. She had made her first voyage to the East in 1800, with successive voyages in 1802, 1804, and 1807. On her fifth voyage, in July, 1810, she was taken in the Mozambique Channel by the French frigate *Bellone* but recaptured in August, off the Ile de France, by the boats of the *Sirius*. The upshot was that she was sent back to England, where she arrived on October 19th, 1811. After refit, the *Windham* was taken up by the Transport Board and did not sail for the East again until February, 1816. The intervening time was mostly spent in a voyage, under Walters' guidance, to Australia.

During this voyage Walters made use of a copy of *The Naval Gazetteer; or Seaman's complete Guide* by John Malham, 2 vols., 2nd edition, bought by him in March, 1810. To this he added some notes of his own, including a workmanlike sketch of " A Rudder for a Ship of the line." In a flyleaf, now detached and torn, he wrote:

SHAKESPEARE.

> Who steals my purse, steals trash,
> 'Tis something, nothing;
> 'Twas mine, 'tis his—and hath been
> Slaves to thousands.
> But he that filches from me my good Name
> Robs me of that which not enriches him
> But makes me poor indeed.

Windham at sea in the South Atlantic Ocean
in Latitude 40° 12′ S
　Longitude 2° 51′ W　which is the
situation of Gough's Island as laid down in
Malham's Naval Gazeteer—having run in its
parallel of Latitude from Longitude 32° 24′
West to 2° 51′ without discovering it,
therefore judge its existence doubtful.([1])

20th December, 1815
S. Walters.

In a manuscript book already described (see page 106) he wrote an extract, in translation, of the letter written by Napoleon to the Prince Regent from the *Bellerophon*, in August, 1815. He finishes with the following:

IN FRANCE.

On his leaving his friends to embark, he said " I would not go without seeing you. We shall never meet again." (it's said). The other, unable to speak, burst into tears ! Bonaparte put his hands on his shoulders and said " In great events we should always display courage and not sensibility."—[this] with an air of affection. Poor fellow. He deserved a better fate—at least an exile in some part of Europe.

SRETLAW LEUMAS.
However, it was the will of
unerring judgment.—Amen.

[1] Gough Island exists all right, in about Lat. 40° 10′ S Long. 9° 50′ W. *Malham's Naval Gazeteer* seems to have been slightly at fault.

Walters' account of the *Windham's* voyage is otherwise given only in tabular form, as follows:

Employed as Agent for Transports and hoisted my pendant in the ship *Windham*. Mr. William Blyth, master, at Deptford, 14th May, 1813.

1813.

	Remarks.	Arrived at	1813. Remarks.
Sail'd from Deptford, 10th June............	Convoy H.M. Ships *Akbar* and *Iris*............	Gravesend................	Same day.
Sail'd from Gravesend, 2nd August............	Embarked 46 Regiment, Colonel Molle, for N.S. Wales, Sydney, with the Brazil and Cape of Good Hope Convoys	Spithead	10th August.
Sail'd from Spithead, 23rd August		Madeira	8th September.
Sail'd from Madeira, 14th September		Rio de Janeiro	13th November.
Sail'd from Rio de Janeiro, 2nd December ...	Port Jackson off Hobart Town, Vandiemans Land. Embarked the 73rd Regiment,	Sydney Cove	11th February, 1814.
Sail'd from Sydney Cove, 14th April	Colonels O'Connell and A.G. [?]...............	River Derwent	21st April.

2nd February, 1814, made the Land S.W. Cape Vandiemans. Same day spoke *Britannia*, ship from Calcutta with convicts. Capn. Hughes, 24th Regiment—the guard, &c., &c., for Sydney Cove.

1814.

	Remarks.	Arrived at	1814. Remarks.
Sail'd from River Derwent, 5th June	7th August went thro' Dampiers Strait. New Britain and Ireland.	Samarang, Isle of Java.	25th August

27th July passed through St. Georges Channel between New Britain and New Ireland.

17th August thro Straights Salaya and anchord off Bolocombe Coast of Celebes.

	Remarks.	Arrived at	Remarks.
Sail'd from Samarang, 12th September.......	Ceylon.................	Point de Gall	29th October.

Passed Straights of Sunda, 15th September, 1814.

1815.

	Remarks.	Arrived at	1815. Remarks.
Sail'd from Colombo, 21st January............	Ships in comy. *Genl. Hewett*, *Upton Castle* joined co. two whalers, *Countess* and *London Town*...............	Cape of Good Hope...	27th March.
Sail'd from Table Bay, 6thMay		St. Helena	20th May.
Sail'd from St. Helena, 4th June............			7th August passed Torbay, the day the Ex Emperor, poor Bonaparte, shifted from the *Bellerophon* to the *Northumberland* for St. Helena.

16th July, 1815, passed the Isle of Flores, Western Islands, and sent boat on shore to get intelligence. Arrived at Spithead the 9th August.

	Remarks.	Arrived at
Sail'd from Spithead, 13th August	Arrived River Thames, Woolwich, and haul'd down the Agent's Pendant, i.e., Discharged from the Transport Service, 15th September, 1815.	Two complete years 4 Lunar months and one week.

Hence the *Wyndham* Transport bore my pendant for thirty lunar months and two weeks, voyage to New South Wales.

With the paying off of the *Windham* on 15th September, 1815, Lieutenant Walters' naval career came to an end. The Navy was being drastically reduced after the peace and the Transport service with it. The 37 lieutenants employed in 1814-1815 were reduced to 25 in the following year and Walters was one of those dispensed with. He was to remain on half-pay until his death in 1834. Of his life during those years all too little is known. After, presumably, a visit to Devonshire, he evidently stayed with his brother in London. The following instructions for varnishing drawings and water-colours were given him by Miles, whose name (playfully reversed) stands at the foot in Samuel's handwriting. This recipe serves to fix his whereabouts in December, 1815, and suggests that Miles—whose turn it was, perhaps, to sympathise with Samuel, poor fellow—was teaching him some of the tricks of the trade. It was perhaps at this period that Samuel's memoirs were being written or copied from earlier notes. The recipe runs as follows:

MEMO.

The procefs to make size, and the method of laying it on, and how to varnish drawings done with water colours on paper.

The picture being complete, to prepare the size is as follows. Take as much parchment as you can hold in your hand openly, and put a little more than half a pint of water; boil it until reduced to one half that quantity; it will be found to be of a glutinous substance, but if too stiff, by adding a little more water will cause it to become pliant; by trying it betwixt the finger and thumb you can judge of it how it will answer. Lay it on by working the brush lightly on the picture. Be careful *not* to use it above milk warm—should it be hotter it will run the colours. Size twice over and let it remain to dry one hour between each time, but should it not be perfectly dry in the hour, let it remain until it is quite so ere the second coat is applied. Remember before the picture is varnished that the size is quite hard. It should have three coats of varnish and have three hours elapse between each coat, which will cause it to have a beautiful glofs.

N.B.—White Hart Spirits of Varnish—in London about 1/3 per gill. The brush should be two and a half inches wide, quite flat—what is termed by limners, sky brushes; any druggist or chemist deals in it, and can be had accordingly.

Poplar. Decr. 1815

Selim Sretlaw.   Mile End.

One may imagine Samuel as busied with his hobby for a year or two, occasionally visiting his friends and relatives. In 1819 his mother died at what is now called Princetown. She died on the 10th of March, Samuel being present or arriving soon afterwards. Mrs. Walters had gone to live on Dartmoor, joining her husband, at some date unknown. Her daughter and son-in-law, Henrietta and John Rodd, were also there from at any rate 1814 until the time of Mrs. Walters' death. There were, up to that time, five children by this marriage, and the grandmother must, in her last years, have been very much surrounded by them. But Dartmoor must have been a queer, desolate place to live in. It had been crowded with prisoners and buzzing with activity while the war continued—there had even been that unfortunate affair in 1814 when the troops had rather needlessly fired on the prisoners of war in a moment of exasperation or panic. Then the Americans were released in 1815 and the last of the French in February of the following year. With their going and the withdrawal of the troops, the whole vast place lay silent and deserted, Princetown becoming " a village of grass-grown highways, closed shops and houses falling into ruin." A Committee of the House of Commons reported in 1818 that the buildings would decay if untenanted much longer. The construction of a horse-tramway out from Plymouth in 1818-1823 did not, in itself, solve the problem; and the place was not in fact used again until 1850. In the meanwhile it was kept up by a few caretakers, of whom John Walters may, very possibly, have been one.

Shortly before, or possibly after, Mrs. Walters' death, Samuel made a wash drawing of her and wrote on the back of it: " Mary de Vassaille Walters, Obit.—10 March, 1819—Born, 13 April, 174-. A real Christian loving tender Mother and a generous friend to all." At about the same time, his mind running, perhaps, on matters of ancestry, he copied out an extract from Gwillam's Heraldry; the arms of Sir William Walters of Saresden, Bart., " descended from the ancient Family of the Walters, of Warwickshire." This wistful entry in his book—sufficiently irrelevant to a Devonshire family which bore no arms and came from somewhere in Wales—shows a hint of that early longing he may have had for social position. He may, at this point, have remembered his mother saying " Do not be so vain!" some thirty years before. At any rate, his mood had changed when, in May, 1819, he wrote the following thoughts on the vanity of wealth and honours. Both, he knew, were beyond his grasp.

TO BE RICH IS NOT TO BE HAPPY ?

And the reality is far from them. Though clothed with grandeur, enriched with wealth, and heaped with honours, who can tell what the mind sustains ? The passions are foes to happinefs, (which) with tranquillity only can dwell; and tranquillity is only to be obtained by peace of mind, the price of which is virtue.

A conscience void of offence will render a person indifferent to evils of life and easy under them; but a troubled conscience, who can bear? It will hourly disturb our repose, will break in on us even in our most festive moments, and destroy every pleasure. It will also render heavier our misfortunes by suggesting to us that they are the consequences of our guilt, and the just punishment of our offences. To observe the golden rule, to do to others as we would be done to— in every instance whatever—will give quiet to our minds and ease our hearts. The satisfaction arising to us from our knowing we have done that which is right is undescribable. It is the only thing that will enable us to support our- selves under afflictions, and it will also add a relish to every pleasure. To bear with patience is a mark of a great mind, but it is no lefs the characteristic proof of an innocent one; for, without that, I think it is almost impossible to be perfectly resigned. Without innocence, vain is the power either of philosophy or religion; while we bear that within us that defeats the powers of both. To silence this monitor is to repent of our crimes, to amend our lives, and to make restitution as far as in us lies, to all we have injured. This, I am aware, is a hard matter, and it will perhaps be argued that what we have suffered for, we have a right to keep. But I deny this; not if you would obtain happinefs. And for that desirable blefsing what price can be too great—even for earthly happinefs, much more for Heavenly? Indeed, one is both, for the former necefsarily in- cludes innocence, and that occasions the latter happinefs for ever, to eternity. This can be purchased by sinners on no other terms but repentance, not merely in words but in actions. A mere form of repentance is nothing—it must be real. Then need he not fear either torment of mind, or of body, which is threatened in the next life, but anticipate the contrary and remain afsured of everlasting blifs.

Dartmoor,   S. W.
3rd May, 1819.

It may be doubted whether the family remained for long on Dartmoor after Mrs. Walters' death. It would be reasonable to suppose, though evidence is scanty, that John Walters and the Rodd family soon moved either to Plymouth or to Lynton (on the coast between Ilfracombe and Minehead), perhaps accompanied by Samuel. The Rodds were at Plymouth in 1831 when their last child (Samuel Miles) was born. John Walters is believed to have died in about 1826, and Samuel evidently inherited from him a house in Plymouth, presumably that in which he had lived. This was No. 6 Bounds Place, Mile Bay, where Samuel himself was living in 1830. Bounds Place still exists and so does the house, though it might be rash to assume that the numbering has remained unaltered. Samuel was still, and was to remain, a bachelor, and his will, drawn up in 1830, bequeathes the house and all else he possessed to his sister, Henrietta Rodd (See Appendix D).

How Samuel Walters spent his years on half-pay is something of a mystery. There exists, however, among the Walters' descendants, a picture of a ship called the *Caroline*, which he is said to have commanded. The likelihood is that he spent many of these years at sea in the merchant service, making his home with the Rodds between each voyage. It was quite usual for half-pay officers to accept such employment with the Admiralty's consent. In asking their Lordships' approval the officer had to specify the tonnage and destination of the vessel, and permission was often withheld on the grounds that she was no fit command for a commissioned officer. Although no correspondence of this kind has so far been found, it is quite possible that a more careful search in the Public Record Office might reveal, as a matter of family interest, something to throw light on his career between 1815 and 1833. From the age of 37 to the age of 55 he should have been quite active. John Rodd was also at sea but mainly perhaps in coastal waters and without (one may suspect) any great financial success.

One characteristic of Samuel Walters was his strong family feeling, which his brothers and sisters shared. It was this which kept him in touch with his elder sister Myra, whom he can hardly have seen since 1795. She had been with her husband at Montreal since 1814, but his death had left her a widow in 1818. She married again in 1824, her second husband being George Savage, a watchmaker and a migrant from Huddersfield. Him, too, she outlived, she herself surviving until 1866. In the meanwhile, however, John Dyde, the elder son by her first marriage, after an adventurous youth, had married in 1822 and become Inspector of Ashes (that is, of potash) at Quebec in 1831, and soon afterwards Manager of the Towboat Company. He was also in the Militia and destined to rise to the rank of Colonel before his distinguished career was ended by death in 1886. In 1832 he was not as important in Canada as he was destined to become, but he was already in a position to help his English relatives should they migrate overseas. No doubt at his mother's suggestion, he seems to have invited Henrietta and John Rodd to Canada, no doubt with the idea of finding a post for Rodd in the towboat business—the early application of the steamboat to the traffic of the St. Lawrence. That the Rodds' move to Canada was intended to be permanent is thus highly probable. But Samuel Walters, who decided to go with them, may possibly have planned to return. The difficulty here is to fathom the mystery of the grant of land of which family tradition makes him the recipient. Land in Canada was being granted quite extensively at this time, especially to men who had been in the armed forces. That Walters should have been given a grant of land is, in itself, quite probable. To set against this, the fact that he apparently retained his house in Plymouth might be thought to indicate an intention to return there; in which case, his acceptance of the grant might have been primarily in the Rodds' interest. Whatever the truth of this, the story of this grant has come down in every branch of the family. According to the late Mr. Gordon Walters Macdougall, K.C., who investigated the matter on the Canadian side in 1896, the grant was made but allowed to lapse through failure to occupy it or pay the taxes. As the land in question is believed to be in the centre of what is now the City of Ottawa, a rueful note creeps into family reminiscence on this subject. John Rodd was no farmer and may not have been interested.

Samuel Walters, John and Henrietta Rodd, and five of the Rodd children, appear to have sailed from England early in 1833. They sailed in the barque *Mint* which, according to the *Quebec Gazette*, landed 121 passengers at Quebec on July 4th. Captain Rodd was at first given the command of the Quebec Steamboat Company's Barge *Hesione*, rigged as a three-masted schooner; later being given a towboat on the St. Lawrence. What Samuel Walters did in Canada is not very clear, except that he voyaged between Montreal and Quebec and visited what was now a large circle of his elder sister's relatives. A letter (in the possession of Mrs. Sutherland Horn, of Vancouver) is almost the only clue to this period of his life and is therefore worth quoting in full:—

Miss Mary Walters Rodd
  c/o John Dyde Esq.
    Steam Packet Quebec, Que.

Montreal, 15 October, 1833.

DEAR MARY,

Your respected father being about to proceed for Quebec in *Croesus* induces me to send you a few lines in order that you may not suspect that no one here save your parents, brothers, and sisters cares about you. I therefore in order to assure you to the contrary, as long as you merit it, shall be always glad and always ready not only to write a commonplace letter, but to give any advice that I conceive you are ready to follow. These I trust will find you and all the dear family of Dydes in the enjoyment of that bountiful blessing, health. For he that has it, has everything with it, and he that is so miserable as to lack it, wants everything to comfort him without the least chance of feeling the smallest relief of his sufferings.

All your dear relatives and friends here are in good health except your poor dear mother, who has been very much afflicted, and is now very low and poorly. I thank Almighty God, with his Divine Aid, for the skill and kindness of Mr. Alfred Savage—who I am forever obliged to, not only for his administering his aid but moreover for that kind manner in which his urbanity prompts him to afford it. He has several times brought her about again into comparative health. She is I am happy to say much better, and the God of all comfort we trust will restore her once more to that usefulness in her humble sphere, which gladdens the hearts of all her relatives here, and I am assured will tend to make you all the happier in Quebec.

Betsey has been somewhat indisposed, occasioned by over-exertions in attending to her mother as well as doing the needful in providing for the family below. Ellen is still very weak in her poor knee, and cannot adventure to do much—consequently the brunt of exertion rests with poor Elizabeth.

Your dear Aunt Savage is as usual mild, meek and apparently easy, and, with slight complaints at intervals, seems to be cheerful if not quite happy. Dear Mr. Savage is always even, uniform and agreeable—full of sensible sallies which greatly enhance the value of his agreeable society and enlivens those whose spirits are not quite so brisk. Edwin is well, but I wish I could add settled to our wishes. I cannot form any idea of his employer's arrangements and really I wish he were in some other situation. However, he had better remain where he is than leave ere he can get other employment. I wish Mr. Dyde could anyway recommend him to a situation as an assistant clerk, or in any mercantile House in Quebec—he is of a promising turn and I trust would give satisfaction—John and Samuel are as usual in perfect health and full of play—always at play, eating or sleeping.

My dear Mary, I have given your mother a trifle of cash to enclose to you [and] hope it will be of service to you. We are all well except your mother, and our prayers are offered to the Throne of Mercy for a continuance of the same blessings to both absent and present friends. All the Savages, Farrs and Rodds desire kind remembrances—and best wishes to all relatives and friends at Quebec.

And believe me to remain, my dear Niece,
Your truly affectionate Uncle,
Samuel Walters.

Samuel's later manner, as an uncle, was on the heavy side. His sister Henrietta, about whose health he is here so worried, was to outlive him, in point of fact, by twenty-seven years. Indeed, from the point of view of "that bountiful blessing, health," Samuel's voyage to Canada was unfortunately timed. For he was still there for the epidemic of 1834. It began in Quebec on the 5th July, the garrison being confined to barracks on the 7th. Dr. Lyons, of the Hospital, King's Wharf, presently diagnosed "Asiatic Cholera of a very malignant character." It was thought to have come from Ireland, brought by vessels which arrived at the Quarantine Station in May and June after losing " a very large proportion " of their passengers. The deaths reported in Quebec rose from 87 in the week July 7th-13th to a maximum of 270 in the week of July 21st-27th. After August 15th the epidemic at Quebec diminished. It had spread, however, along the St. Lawrence and raged afresh at Montreal. Samuel Walters was among the victims, dying on 29th July and being buried on the same evening in Papineau Cemetery by the Minister of Zion, First Congregational Church of Montreal. Even so, his relatives managed to print a funeral notice during the day, which remains the only clue to where he had been living. It reads:

SIR,

You are requested to attend the Funeral of the late Lieut. Samuel Walters, R.N., from his residence, No. 3, St. Henry Street, to the place of interment (New Burying Ground), at Seven o'clock this evening.

Montreal, Tuesday, July 29, 1834.

At any other time his death would have been marked by some obituary notice in the local press. But the epidemic was too serious and burials too frequent for anything but statistics of mortality and incomplete lists of reported victims. Apart from the Admiralty's removal of his name from the List of Sea Officers, his death was noticed only in the *Gentleman's Magazine*, Part 1, for 1835; and then but in one line stating briefly his death " at Quebec." His property was left, as we have seen, to Henrietta Rodd. When she died his bones were moved to a grave adjacent to hers in Mount Royal Cemetery. A number of relics of Samuel Walters have survived; notably, two books (see page 106 and page 111), his sword, spectacles, and sea-chest, in the possession of Mr. Frank Walters Mills, of Pointe Claire, Quebec, and his sword-knot in the possession of Mrs. Isolene (Rodd) Kendall, of Berkeley, California. He has been well remembered among the descendants of his nephews and nieces, more especially in Canada; and if brought up to believe that he fought at Trafalgar they have not been, after all, so far from the truth.

What is one to say, finally, of his character ? Evidence hardly suffices to judge with any degree of confidence, but what there is seems fairly consistent. He began life with fair ability, good character, and some desire to see the world. He had enough energy and ambition to gain an advancement which his earlier bookish tastes would scarcely have foreshadowed. He proved a competent seaman, an excellent navigator, a valuable officer of the watch and no coward in action. With the position, however, of 1st Lieutenant he had probably reached, possibly exceeded, the limits of his capacity for command. There is no knowing what a further spell of that heavier responsibility might have done for his character. But his own account leaves the reader with no certainty that a further opportunity would have led to a greater degree of success. In particular, his attempt to cut out the Indiaman on 3rd January, 1810 (see page 94)—perhaps the best chance of distinction he ever had—was as unimpressive in style as in result. Here a certain significance might be allowed to his writing " This was the plan agreed upon by myself and the officers appointed for this service." This is not the language of a man with any real grip on the situation. He, after all, was in command. It was for him to explain, not to discuss, his plan. It was for him to impress his subordinates with his determination to carry it out. But he betrays, in his account, a doubt as to whether the plan was even practicable; and any doubt on his part would have proportionately weakened the resolution of the men he led. The boats failing to keep together—" but it might be all for the best "—the flotilla never reached an attacking position. Walters decided that the operation had failed and " with the concurrence of Lieut. Dwyer " set about collecting the scattered boats. Again, there is a note of consultation rather than command. No one could say, on available evidence, whether greater determination could have led to a different result, but it is worthy of note that his own barge, by itself, could have delivered an attack of sorts, provided only that it neared the objective with a single fireboat in tow. He ends his narrative with a half-expressed doubt as to whether the rear boats had really been trying. From all this the reader has no grounds for doubting his courage, but some reason for questioning his powers of command. It seems possible that his final position, as third lieutenant in a ship of the line, fairly represented the Navy's assessment of his quality. He lacked, perhaps, the ruthless touch by which the born leader is, in the last resort, to be distinguished. He showed up to better advantage, especially as a navigator, in the *Windham's* voyage to Australia; it was no passage for the inexperienced or the unskilled.

If the reader of his memoirs may hazard a further guess as to his character— and the editor of this volume is in no position to judge more truly than anyone else who has read it—he might conclude that Walters' self-distrust arose from two inconsistent elements in his mind. He combined social ambition with a nonconformist outlook. The Samuel Walters who thought in youth of becoming a gentleman, who memorised the French and Latin tags which might prove useful, who wistfully copied out the coat-armour of another Walters' family (with which his own was unconnected) had no business to be frequenting the chapel as well. Or, to put it the other way round, the staid moralist who renounced riches and vanity should not, in writing his memoirs, have been at pains to seem of better education than he was. His portrait, moreover, would seem to reveal a sensitiveness, a diffidence which, while giving promise of distinction, would hardly suggest a career as a man of action. It was, one feels, as an artist that he was most truly himself. And several of his drawings show a delicacy of line that amounts, surely, to something more than competence. There can be little doubt that his artistic gifts, if developed sooner, would have been very respectable.

Whatever there was of the artist in him appeared later in a nephew of the same name. His story, one of relative failure, is incomplete, therefore, without reference to that later Samuel Walters in whom the family potentialities were at length fulfilled. Called after Lieutenant Walters, the younger Samuel was born at sea, as already noted, in 1811, and baptised, it is thought, at Spittalfields, Middlesex. He had two elder brothers and one younger sister and was probably brought up, like the eldest, William, to be a frame-maker and gilder. But he must soon have shown a preference for drawing and painting, in which he evidently owed much to the artistic leanings of his father and uncle. In about 1825 he moved with his father to Liverpool, where his eldest brother set up business as a frame-maker and gilder in Bold Street, and where his father, in 1834, was living at 11, Dunkin Street, Great George Street. To quote from Samuel's obituary in the *Liverpool Mercury:*

> He was born in London in the year 1811, but when quite young came to Liverpool where he commenced as a portrait painter, and in that line promised to be very successful, but was drawn into marine work through his father being engaged in that line of art in a very modest way. His success as a marine painter is well known both in Liverpool and the United States, where many of his pictures went. . . . He was a student, and also at one time a member, of the Liverpool Academy. . . .

In 1835 Samuel married Betsey, fourth daughter of Mr. Michael Pilley. Nine of his children lived beyond infancy, of whom George Stanfield Walters (born 1 December, 1837) was eldest. Some of his earlier Liverpool pictures date from about 1836. He appears in the Census of 1851 as resident at 56, Stanhope Street, Liverpool, with a family of six between the ages of 2 and 13—two others having died within a few days of each other in December, 1839, The fact that Maria Walters was born about 1847 at Hackney, Middlesex, suggests that the family had at least one period of residence in London. It is believed that Samuel Walters lived at one time in the Kingsland Road and rented a studio in Leadenhall Street, right among the shipping fraternity which formed his public. His painting of the *Great Eastern* off Margate in 1857 dates presumably from that period of his life. But Liverpool must have afforded as good a market and, after about 1865, probably a better. He was back there, at any rate, in 1858 and his picture " The Burning of the clipper ship *James Baines* in the Huskisson Dock " may serve to date his return. With growing fame and prosperity, he could afford to live in quieter surroundings and it was now, perhaps, that he went to live at 76, Merton Road, Bootle. He went on painting until his death on March 5th, 1882, from cancer and heart disease, and was buried at Anfield Cemetery (General Section, grave 390). His wife outlived him and was resident at 20, Weld, Birkdale, when she died in 1901.

Samuel Walters' fame as a painter is firmly established and rests not on obituary notices and local traditions but upon the lasting merit of his work. Many of his pictures have survived and are highly valued, notably " The Rival, off Rio " and " The *Gypsy*, outward bound, off New Brighton," both in the Liverpool Museum. His famous " Port of Liverpool " is in the Walker Art Gallery, Liverpool, and other examples of his work are to be seen in the Picture Gallery, Boston, U.S.A. A number of his pictures are in the offices of the Cunard, Pacific, and other lines and there are a great number in private hands, several in the possession of Mr. Ernest Royden. Others belong to the painter's descendants and to private purchasers in the United States. A public exhibition of his work in Liverpool is long overdue.

The following extract from the *Illustrated London News* of March 25th, 1882, shows at once his contemporary standing as a painter and the degree in which his skill was inherited by his eldest son:—

> The death of Mr. Samuel Walters, of Bootle, Liverpool, an artist well known for his many excellent pictures of ships and other paintings, was announced last week. His works have gained high reputation in America as well as in England; one being that of the ill-fated steam-ship *President*, which picture was engraved and dedicated by permission to Martin Van Buren, then President of the United States. His last picture, upon which he was at work within a few days of his death, was a delineation of the fine steamer *Parisian*, belonging to Messrs. Allan and Co. In his studio he leaves numerous sketches and other works, which when offered to the public will be no doubt eagerly sought after. Among them is the fine picture of the " Port of Liverpool," which is well known by the photographs taken from it and widely distributed. Of late years most of his pictures have been reproduced by photography and sent all over the world. His eldest son, Mr. George S. Walters, also known as an artist, is settled in London, but for many years lived in Bootle and worked with his father, to whom he owes his training in the profession. We present a portrait of the late Mr. Samuel Walters, from a photograph by Mr. W. Keith of Lord Street, Liverpool.

George Stanfield Walters was educated at Liverpool Grammar School, but worked in his father's studio from the age of 14 or 15, mainly in painting in the rigging of ship-portraits. He worked at first in Liverpool but had evidently moved to London before his father died. He was a member of the Royal Society of British Artists and the Langham Sketching Club, exhibiting at the Royal Academy and in most London exhibitions (and chiefly in Suffolk Street) between 1860 and 1893. He died in 1924. Many of his works are still extant, including four of his drawings in the British Museum. It was he who applied for a coat-of-arms, receiving the arms of Walters of Devonshire: Or a Lion rampant sable pierced with two swords in saltire proper. Crest: A dove holding an olive branch proper. Motto, in Welsh: "Fy Num A Cymru" meaning "My God and Wales." His great-uncle would have liked that.

What is most significant, perhaps, in this family history is the hereditary process by which a great marine painter gained his skill. An intelligent builder, probably able to draw plans of buildings, has two sons, both probably trained as carpenters and shipwrights. One goes to sea (possibly) and then becomes a carver and gilder. The other has ability enough to make himself a naval officer but not quite the character for complete success in war. He has, instead, a marked artistic talent and learns something of the technical side from his brother, who also paints. They both, naturally, prefer to paint what they understand—that is, ships. The son of the carver and gilder, nephew of the sailor, is encouraged by the example of his father and uncle to do painting and nothing else. Beginning early enough, he learns how to use his brushes and then—uniting in himself something of the inherited aptitudes of the draughtsman, the shipwright, the carver, and the sailor—is able to become one of the leading marine painters of the day. His maturity coincides with a shipping boom which provides him with clients. His skill is transmitted to a second generation with some few traces appearing in a third, and then the impetus dies away, probably for ever. Marine painting more or less died out, after all, with the sailing ship.

This is not to say that the Walters' family has not produced other distinguished men—for it has—but their ability has lain in other directions. And what future distinction the younger Walters of to-day may achieve will again be different and will result, very likely, from such a convergence of inherited abilities as produced Samuel Walters the painter. The descendants of Miles Walters are numerous in the Liverpool area—a vast number of people of that name must be descended either from Samuel Walters or from his brother William. The descendants of Myra and Henrietta Walters—the Dydes, MacDougalls, Mills, Rodds, and Cribbs—are numerous in Canada, where also one of the Liverpool family, Mr. Percy R. Walters of Montreal, is exceedingly well known in the tobacco-trade. The Walters flourish on both sides of the Atlantic and wherever else they chance to be. They are a good family.

But how, it will be asked, did the elder Samuel Walters' book of memoirs come to be found at New Orleans ? That was, at the outset, the hardest problem of all; and a problem for long it remained. In the first place, however, it was safe to assume that his sister Henrietta (Mrs. Rodd) inherited it under his will. Actually, as it transpired, she inherited not only the manuscript but the diary-keeping habit as well. And it is from her diary that the manuscript's wanderings can, at least by inference, be traced. Captain John Rodd was a towboat master on the St. Lawrence when Lieutenant Walters died. He was the father, it will be remembered, of a large family of which Elizabeth Rebecca (born 1814) was—unfortunately for her—the eldest, and Edwin Walters (born 1816) the second child and eldest son. It was of him that Samuel wrote (see page 119), " Edwin is well, but I wish I could add settled to our wishes. . . . I wish Mr. Dyde could anyway recommend him to a situation as an assistant clerk . . . he is of a promising turn. . . ." Samuel's judgment on his 17-year-old nephew was sound, but Edwin's immediate ideas were, apparently, different. He seems to have gone to sea. What was to prove his last voyage, however, ended in 1836 at New Orleans, where his ship was detained indefinitely for lack of cargo and the crew, naturally, discharged. Edwin, thus left on the beach, found employment with Mr. John Hall, a sugar and molasses merchant. Despite his own first preference—which he may by this time have come to regret—the assistant clerkship had come his way and he gave all the satisfaction that his uncle had said he would. He prospered sufficiently to marry a girl from Cardiff in 1836, and then take her to meet his parents at Montreal in the following year. Captain Rodd was still towing vessels and log-rafts about the St. Lawrence, but this led to an accident in the *Bytown* towboat on May 27th, 1841. It looks as if the capable Henrietta took over the accounts during his temporary incapacity and entered them—perhaps for want of another ledger—on a blank leaf or two of her brother's manuscript memoirs. The book was still in her possession, at any rate, in 1841. John Rodd soon recovered but, with lessened enthusiasm for towage, became master of a ferry-boat called the *Princess Victoria* which operated between Montreal and Laprairie. This occupation being seasonal, a frozen St. Lawrence gave him and his wife the leisure for a trip to visit Edwin in the winter of 1843-44 and see a fairly numerous brood of grandchildren. The following extract from Henrietta's diary is in itself a tribute to the communications by then established with the United States, which evidently showed a marked improvement since the days of General Burgoyne:—

ACCOUNT OF TRIP BY CAPT. RODD AND HIS WIFE, HENRIETTA (WALTERS) RODD, TO NEW ORLEANS, LA., TO SEE THEIR SON, EDWIN WALTERS RODD AND HIS FAMILY, IN 1843-44.

Christmas day 25 December, 1843. Left Montreal to proceed to New Orleans, La., at 1 p.m. Arrive in the evening at St. Johns, Que., and spend the night there. Reach Burlington, Vt., next evening, and sleep there. Proceed on and sleep at St. Albans, Vt. Start the next morning for Albany, N.Y. Rode all night, and got to Albany Friday three o'clock in the afternoon. 29th left this morning for New York, N.Y., where we stopped till New Year, 1 January, 1844. Set out by steam boat at 5 a.m., got to Philadelphia, Penn., at 12 o'clock. Set out at 4 o'clock for Baltimore, Md. Rode all night and got there the next day. Slept there, and next morning at 7 o'clock set out by railroad for Wheeling, W.Va. Rode all day by railroad, and in the evening we got in a stage-coach and went all night over the Alleghany mountains. Got to Wheeling, W.Va., at half-past eleven Wednesday night, and stayed till Friday at 10 o'clock at the Virginia Hotel. Sailed by steam-boat, *Little Pike*, under Capt. Mason, for New Orleans. 5th January, got to Portsmouth, Ohio, Saturday 6th. Sunday 7th got to Cincinnati, Ohio, and Covington, and Newport. Finally we arrived all well on Tuesday 16 January, 1844, at New Orleans, La.

It was almost certainly during this visit that Mrs. Rodd handed over her brother's manuscript to her eldest son. Edwin was evidently prospering at New Orleans, and when Grace, his wife, died on 18th October, 1849, he married, after a decent interval, the daughter of his employer, Mr. John Hall. If not already a partner in the firm, his marriage with Catherine Ann Hall in 1851 made him one. His wealth may be judged from the fact that his summer home, burnt in 1858, was valued at $80,000. But Edwin was destined to see troubled times in Louisiana. The American Civil War, which helped, in the end, to enrich his cousins in Liverpool, was no prosperous time for the merchants of the blockaded Confederate States. Apart from that, many of his sons (he had five children by his first wife and nine by his second) must have served in the army. It is this period which is represented in the manuscript volume by the engraved bazaar ticket. " Southern Hospital Association " it reads, " New Orleans. Bazaar, Feb. 18th, 1867. Tickets One Dollar each. J. B. Hood, Pres't." It bears in the middle a lifelike picture of a southern lady handing refreshment to a wounded Confederate soldier.

Edwin Rodd's eldest son was called John Edwin and began in business with his father. Following the death of his first wife, within a few months of their marriage, John Edwin joined the Confederate army and was badly wounded at Fredericksburg. Surviving the war, nevertheless, he married again in 1870, just before his father died, and spent the rest of his life in New Orleans. The decade or so after the southern defeat was a depressing period, no doubt, in the history of Louisiana. The emancipation of the negroes had disorganized the whole economic structure of the region and it was perhaps in an atmosphere of commercial depression that buildings were allowed to decay and offices left desolate and unkept. The wounded and defeated Confederate soldier John Edwin Rodd may have cared little enough for the manuscript volume he had inherited. It was he, evidently, who lost sight of it as he grew older, perhaps leaving it behind in an office he had formerly used. As an old man he had ceased, perhaps, to bother about things, more especially after his wife's death in 1910. He showed, it may be, no interest when the demolition began of the old offices he must once have known. The arrival of the S.S. *Naperian* had no interest for him either. And when she sailed again he was not to know—and might not even have cared—that Mr. Neligan had in his cabin on board her the manuscript here transcribed, to the chance discovery of which this book must owe its origin, its substance and its end.

APPENDIX A

ADMIRALS.	SHIPS.	CAPTNS.	ENTRY.	DISCHARGE.	
Earl St. Vincent...	Argo [44]....	James Bowen	April 19th. 1798	April 1802....	
I. F Duckworth..	Monkey [14]....	Henry Weir ..... James Tillard.... Wm. Tatham....	April 1802....	Septr 1803....	15 years in the Regular Service.
	Goliath [74]..	Chas. Brisbane..	24th Novr 1804	March 1805.	
R. Adml. Bertie...	Raisonable [64]	Robt. Barton..... Josias Rowley.... Robt. Corbet.... Jms. Hatley.....	9th March 1805	31st July 1810	
	Courageux [74]	P. Wilkinson	24th Novr 1810	March 1813	
	Windham	Arm'd .... 22 guns .... 878 tons .... Transport .... I Andrews .. Wm. Blythe...... Owner...... Master........			2½ years on Staff & P Service.
	Lt. Walters	Agent	14 May 1813	15th Sept 1815	
Honble Sir Wm Cornwallis Channel [Fleet] V Aml. England. (¹)	Ville de Paris [100]	TR Ricketts TLM Gosselin John Whitby	Sept 1803	24th Nov 1804	17 years constantly employed at sea & 2½ years in the Ocean India man Capt John Bowen 1796. making 20 years service at sea from the last date. Sept. 1815. S.W.
	Rear Admiral Sir Wm. Domett Capn. of ye Fleet This list of the Ville de Paris should have been placed next the Monkey.	Argo [44] Monkey [14] Ville de Paris [110] Goliath [74] Raisonable [64] Courageux 74 Guns 380 Isle of France, Bournbon & East Indies.	Channel, Mediterranean, Madeira, Down Coast Africa, North Sea; Coast of Holland Channel blockading the French Fleet in Brest. Ditto Ireland, Bantry Bay, Bear Haven. Channel, Cape of Good Hope, Rio De La Plat.		

¹ Commander-in-Chief in the Channel 2nd Vice-Admiral of England. The latter title was an honorary distrinction arising from great seniority. It involved no duties as such.

APPENDIX B

Account of Ships and Colonies Captured of Which the *Raisonable* was present at

OF WHAT NATION.	DATE OF CAPTURE.	REMARKS, &C.	NAMES OF
Spanish	22nd July, 1805.........	In a general action with the combined Squads. of France and Spain.	St. Rafael [74] ⎱ Ell Firme [84] ⎰
„	„		
French	16th August, 1805	By the *Goliath*, *Raisonable* in co.	L'Torche [18].
Dutch	10th January, 1806......	By the Forces under the command of Lieut.- General Sir David Baird and Commodore Sir H. Popham.	Cape of Good Hope
Spanish	28th June, 1806........		Buenos Ayres
„	3rd February, 1807	By General Sir S. Auchmuty and Rear Admiral Stirling.	Monte Video
French Merchant Ship...	10th October, 1808.....	Laden with livestock from the Isle of Madagascar bound to Port S.E.	Le Pasiphae
Having been captd by *L' Manche*, French Frigate in Indian Sea............	28th October, 1808.....	This vefsel belonged to the Squadron in the East Indies.	Seaflower [14]
Lugger, French	21st November	On a cruise.	L'Adventure
Arab	5th December	Cut her out of Rosas Bay after chasing her under the battery where she anchord.	Taze Bax Ship
French Frigate	21st Sept., 1809, captured in St. Paul's Road, Isle Bourbon...	By the Forces under the command of Colonel Keating, 56th Reg., a detachment of that Corps., Bombay Native Infantry, and about three hundred seamen. For particulars read the account in its place.	L'Caroline [44].
English East India Ships..			Streatham (E.I.C.) [30] ⎱ Europe (E.I.C.) [30] ⎰
„ „ „ „			
French			La Fanny, pierced [14]
„			La Trois Amis
„		Suffice it to say it was as enterprising an attack and capture as was made during the late war.	La Creole
„			Grappler [18]
Brig, American............	December	Bound to the Isle of France, breaking laws of blockade.	Charles Merchant
French	21st December	By the *Boadicea* in company.	La Margueritta

AT THE CAPE OF GOOD HOPE.

French .... 4th March, 1806	Came into Table Bay not knowing it was in the possefsion of the English.	*L'Volontaire* [44]
„ .... ditto	ditto.	*Rolla* [14].

RIVER PLATE.

Spanish Schooners .... 27th June, 1806.........	Squadron under Sir H. Popham.	*Belem & Dolores*
„ „ .... 3rd February, 1807	Captured the morning of the storming of Monte	*La Paula* [22]
„ „	Video by General Sir S. Auchmuty and Rear	*La Fuerta* [22]
„ „	Admiral Stirling. All those vefsels were	*La Hero* [10]
„ „	French Cruisers.	*Los Dolores* [10]
„ „	The Merchant vefsels were prizes to French Priva-	*La Paz* [10]
„ „	teers on the Coast of Guinea.	*La Reyna Louisa** [26]
Chiefly English Guinea Ships	N.B.—Gun boats and Merchant Vefsels were all destroyed on White-lock's Failure.	20 Gun boats and upwards of 40 Sail of Merchant Ship-ping. }

* This was the Commodore's Ship.

APPENDIX C.

SUPERIOR COURT
FOR THE
DISTRICT OF MONTREAL

SAMUEL WALTERS, of Montreal, (G. P.) Lieutenant Royal Navy, died on the twenty ninth day of July one thousand eight hundred & thirty four; & was buried on this the twenty ninth day of July one thousand eight hundred & thirty-four.

RICHARD MILES
GEO SAVAGE
EDWARD WHIPPLE

I, THE UNDERSIGNED, DEPUTY PROTHONOTARY of the Superior Court for the District of Montreal do hereby certify that the foregoing is a TRUE EXTRACT from the duplicate of the register of Civil Status kept by the (First) Congregational Church in the City of Montreal, for the year one thousand eight hundred and thirty-four, now forming part of Archives of the Superior Court for the district of Montreal.

MONTREAL, the twenty-six day of July one thousand nine hundred and forty-eight.

(Signed) P. LALIME,

Deputy Prothonotary of the Superior
Court for the District of Montreal.

APPENDIX D.

BE it remembered that on this twenty-sixth day of August in the year of our Lord one thousand eight hundred and thirty four, at the City of Montreal in the District of Montreal in the province of Lower Canada. Before the Honorable George Pyke one of the Judges of His Majesty's Court of King Bench of and for the said District.—Appeared Henrietta Rodd wife of John Rodd of Montreal Mariner authorized by her said husband also present appearing & consenting, Executrix & universal legatee of the Last Will & Testament hereto annexed dated the fourth day of July one thousand Eight hundred & Thirty—and prayed to be allowed the probate thereof and due proof having been made before me of the said last Will as appears by the depositions of George Savage and Alfred Savage both of Montreal, taken before me and herewith annexed.

I do hereby order and Declare that the said Last Will and Testament be Insinuated and enregistered and Exemplifications granted thereof according to Laws.

Given under my hand & the Seal of the said Court the day & year first above written.

(signed) GEORGE PYKE
J. K. B.

I, the undersigned, do hereby certify that the foregoing Last Will and Testament of the said Samuel Walters and the order touching the Probate of the same are true copies of the originals remaining deposited in the Archives of the Superior Court at Montreal.

Montreal, July 30th, 1948. D. P. S. C.

THE LAST WILL and TESTAMENT
of Lieutenant SAMUEL WALTERS, Royal Navy.

In the name of God Amen. I Samuel Walters of Plymouth in the County of Devonshire, make this my last will and Testament. I resign my soul to its Creator in all humble hope of its future happiness, as in the disposal of a Being infinitely good. As to my Body, that it be buried decently where most convenient. I hereby make and appoint my well beloved Sister Henrietta Rodd Executrix of this my last will and Testament. I give and devise to my Sister Mrs Henrietta Rodd my House situated in bounds place—Mile Bay—No. 6—Plymouth—and everything I possess in this world at the time of my death.

This is my last will and Testament, written with my own Hand, and sealed with my seal this—Fourth day of July—in year of our Lord one thousand eight hundred and Thirty.

(signed) SAMUEL WALTERS

Signed, Sealed, and Declared by the Testator, as his last Will and Testament, in Presence of us,

(Signed) DAVID DAVIS
WILLIAM PRESSLY
JOHN DAVIS

No. 6 Bounds Place, Mile Bay,
Plymouth.

APPENDIX E

CHART 1

DESCENDANTS OF JOHN WALTERS OF ILFRACOMBE, DEVONSHIRE

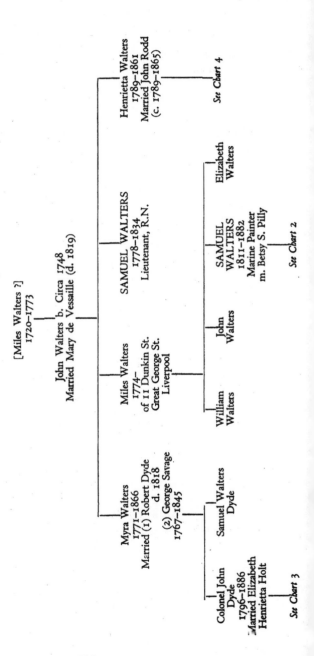

[Miles Walters ?]
1720–1773

John Walters b. Circa 1748
Married Mary de Vessaille (d. 1819)

Myra Walters
1771–1866
Married (1) Robert Dyde
d. 1818
(2) George Savage
1767–1845

Miles Walters
1774–
of 11 Dunkin St.
Great George St.
Liverpool

SAMUEL WALTERS
1778–1834
Lieutenant, R.N.

Henrietta Walters
1789–1861
Married John Rodd
(c. 1789–1865)

See Chart 4

Colonel John
Dyde
1796–1886
Married Elizabeth
Henrietta Holt

See Chart 3

Samuel Walters
Dyde

William
Walters

John
Walters

SAMUEL
WALTERS
1811–1882
Marine Painter
m. Betsy S. Pilly

See Chart 2

Elizabeth
Walters

134

CHART 2

DESCENDANTS OF SAMUEL WALTERS OF LIVERPOOL, MARINE PAINTER

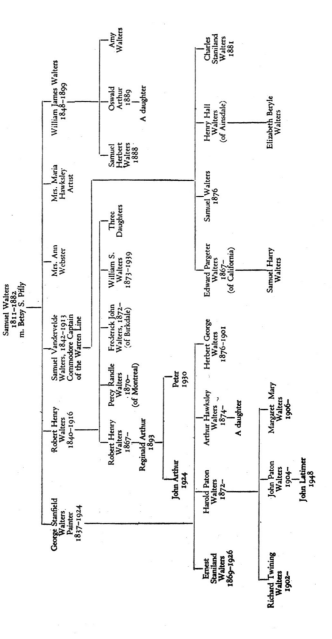

DESCENDANTS OF MYRA WALTERS—THE DYDE FAMILY OF CANADA

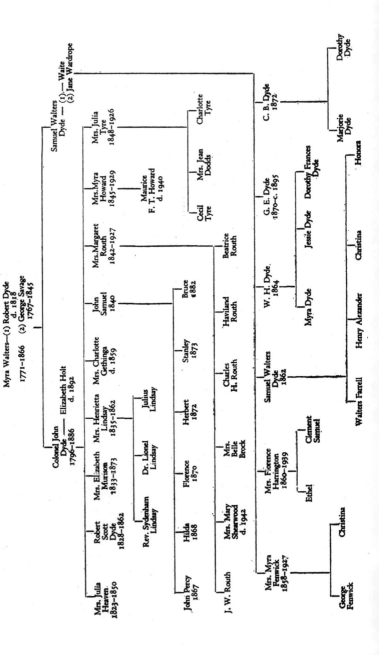

CHART 4

DESCENDANTS OF HENRIETTA WALTERS—THE RODD FAMILY OF CANADA

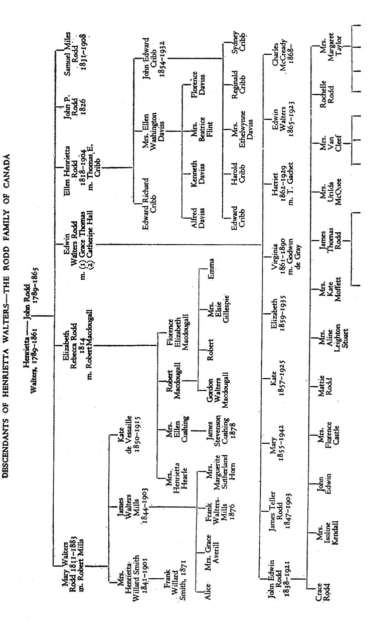

NOTES.

1. A French Squadron had sailed from Brest on 17th September, 1798, consisting of one ship of the line (the *Hoche*), eight frigates, a schooner, and a brig. They were overtaken on the 12th October by Sir John Borlase Warren, whose Squadron captured the *Hoche* and three frigates, namely, *La Bellone* [40], *La Coquille* [40], and *L'Ambuscade* [36]. A detachment of three French frigates had already appeared off the N.W. Coast of Ireland on 22nd August, landing General Humbert with 850 troops at Killala. After an initial success, he surrendered on 8th September to a force under the command of the Marquis Cornwallis.

2. Vice-Admiral Bruix sailed from Brest on 25th April, 1799, with twenty-five sail of the line, successfully evading Lord Bridport's blockading fleet. He entered the Mediterranean, causing Lord Keith to abandon the blockade of Cadiz in order to join the Earl St. Vincent at Gibraltar. Thus released, the Spanish Fleet in Cadiz, seventeen sail of the line, put to sea but, suffering from a gale, took refuge in Carthagena. Earl St. Vincent, who had at first proceeded with his whole fleet to Port Mahon, Minorca, now tried to prevent a junction of the Spanish ships with Bruix, then thought to be at Toulon. He was off Cape San-Sebastian with that object on the 24th May. It was shortly afterwards, on 2nd June, that St. Vincent's health broke down. Handing over the command to Lord Keith, he sailed for Minorca in the *Ville-de-Paris*. There he transferred his flag to the *Argo* [44], in which he sailed for England.

3. In his article on James Bowen in the Dictionary of National Biography Sir John Knox Laughton wrote: "It is told by ancient tradition that on the Admiral giving the order 'Starboard.'' Bowen ventured to say 'My Lord, you'll be foul of the French ship if you dont take care.' 'What is that to you, sir?' replied Howe sharply 'starboard!' 'Starboard!' cried Bowen, muttering by no means inaudibly, 'Damned if *I* care, if *you* dont. I'll

take you near enough to singe your black whiskers.' He did almost literally fulfil this promise, passing so close under the stern of the *Montagne*, that the French ensign brushed the main and mizen shrouds of the *Queen Charlotte*."

4. Many of the British naval achievements of 1793-1815 were made possible by the medical progress made during the previous war and the decade which followed. Credit for this progress must be shared by many, but some, clearly, belongs to Sir Gilbert Blane, Rodney's Physician-of-the-Fleet, many of whose recommendations were put into effect. By 1795 (and, indeed, very largely by 1783) the problems of hygiene and diet in European waters had been more or less solved. No comparable progress had been made in tropical medicine and the local diseases in the East and West Indies continued to take their toll.

5. Calder's action, for the conduct of which he was severely reprimanded by a Court-Martial, had important indirect results. Neither Calder nor Villeneuve tried to renew the action on the 23rd and 24th July, but the latter, in proceeding to Corunna, virtually abandoned the attempt to carry out Napoleon's orders. The concentration in the Channel, as a preliminary to the invasion of England, was now seen to be impracticable. As regards the justice of Calder's treatment, a French author once asked what they would have done to him in England had he commanded—as Villeneuve did—the superior fleet, and had lost two ships instead of taking them ?

6. James, in his *Naval History* (Vol. IV, page 189 of the 1859 edition) states that Sir Home Popham was told by the master of an American merchantman (the *Rolla*) that the inhabitants of Monte Video and Buenos Ayres were " so ridden by their government " that they would offer no resistance to a British Army. He infers that this was Popham's principal reason for planning the expedition. Popham's motives were actually more complex than that. To grasp them, three separate sets of circumstances need to be borne in mind.

(a) Popham was anathema to all orthodox naval officers, and especially to those senior to him. Everything about him was irregular. He was born at Tetuan and partly educated at Cambridge. He had commanded an East Indiaman, not in the Honourable Company's service, but one sailing from Ostend under the Emperor's flag—she had even become a prize to a British frigate. Then, in the Navy, he was promoted for service on land by recommendation of the Duke of York. He was knighted but by the Tsar of Russia and as a Knight of Malta. He knew a number of languages and was a Fellow of the Royal Society. He was intimate with politicians but loathed by Admirals.

(b) Popham, Baird, and Beresford did not meet in 1806 for the first time. With Auchmuty, they were the heroes of the Red Sea Expedition of 1801, a pet project of Henry Dundas which, without achieving a very decisive result, attracted a great deal of public acclaim. They were ready, as a team, to repeat their previous success or improve on it. Apart from that, however, the Red Sea expedition under Popham had been particularly disliked by St. Vincent and his friends as a poaching on the preserves of Admiral Blankett, the man already there. Through having served as a lieutenant to Keppel, Blankett stood high in their estimation. Jeremy Bentham, by contrast, thought him "one of the most wrong-headed blockheads" he had ever encountered. St. Vincent's opinion of Blankett (and of Popham) was likely, however, at this time, to carry more weight.

(c) Cape Town was occupied on 12th January, 1806, and Popham and Beresford sailed from Table Bay for the River Plate on the 14th April. During the intervening months, on February 10th, a change of Ministry had brought in a new Board of Admiralty: Charles Grey, Rear-Admiral Markham, Sir Charles Pole, and Mr. Benjamin Tucker as Second Secretary. It was almost a return of the St. Vincent Board of 1801-1804. For the new Ministry, to supersede Baird and Popham was mere routine, even had these commanders kept to the letter of their orders.

Popham and Baird were, of course, guiltless of any such slavish adherence to the written word. Neither, however, had they succumbed to the influence of an American merchant-seaman. Popham had discussed the River Plate project with Ministers as early as 1803, when he was in close touch with Francisco de Miranda. He had submitted Miranda's plan to Pitt in October, 1804, and believed then that an expedition to South America, under his leadership, had been decided upon.

Action on those lines was then postponed and it was Popham himself (by his own account) who suggested the expedition to the Cape. He claimed afterwards, however, in his defence, that the other plan was still under discussion when he left England.

" On the 29th July, 1805, I took leave of Mr. Pitt, when I had a long conversation with him on the original project of the Expedition to South America; in the course of which Mr. Pitt informed me, that from the then state of Europe and the Confederacy in part formed, and forming, against France, there was a great anxiety to endeavour by friendly negotiation to detach Spain from her connection with that power; and until the result of such an attempt should be known, it was desirable to suspend all hostile operations in South America; but in case of failure in the object, it was his intention again to enter on the Original project . . .

" Death has deprived me of the means of proving the particulars of what pafsed in my last interview with that Illustrious and ever to be lamented Statesman. . . ."

(P.R.O. Ad. 1/5378. Report on Court-Martial.)

Popham always tended to know what Cabinet policy was. "As I said to the Prime Minister . . ." he would explain, in effect, and without gaining much in popularity among his official superiors. Knowing, as he said he did, why the expedition to South America had been postponed, he had no difficulty in showing that the reasons for its postponement no longer held good. After Ulm and Austerlitz, no European confederacy was possible.

". . . I well knew it to be a favourite object of Mr. Pitt—I knew the causes which had suspended it, and I was well satisfied that my having received no Instructions on the subject arose from there being not the most distant idea of those causes being so suddenly removed by the rapid and total change which took place in the state of Europe, from the succefses of Buonaparte." (ibid).

There can be little doubt that the news of Popham's South American escapade would, in fact, have been received by Pitt—had he lived to receive it—without all the sensations felt by St. Vincent's friends. But even Pitt and Dundas would have regretted that the attempt should have been made with so small a force and with troops whose removal would weaken, perhaps dangerously, the garrisons at the Cape and St. Helena. Only an overwhelming success could have wholly justified it.

7. The success of the River Plate expedition turned on the attitude of the South American colonists. It was believed that they were discontented with Spanish rule and on the point of active rebellion. This was perfectly true. They rebelled soon afterwards in 1809. But the influence at work was that of the French Revolution, combined with the example of the United States, and the colonists were in no mood to exchange the rule of Spain for the equally remote (and far more alien) rule of England. The English interests which Pitt mainly represented were intent, it is true, on trade rather than conquest. They retained the Elizabethan desire to supply the Spanish colonies with the goods which Spain herself could never provide. But to this they added a hunger for markets to replace all those lost in occupied Europe. Behind Popham, restrained with difficulty, was a pent-up torrent of unsold textiles and hardware. Nor, when the dam burst, were the South Americans unwilling to buy. What they resented was foreign interference in a Spanish family quarrel coupled with the likelihood of annexation by England. Surprised—as well they might be—by the arrival of the English troops, they yielded Buenos Ayres without much opposition. The Viceroy fled and Beresford sent home 1,086,208 dollars, mainly in specie. He was at pains, simultaneously, to win over the inhabitants by releasing all their shipping and issuing a Proclamation in which he promised to protect their religion and give them "a free trade, and all the advantages of a commercial intercourse with Great Britain, where no oppression exists . . ." It took the colonists about a month to realise that Beresford's forces amounted to less than 1,500 all told, consisting mainly of his own Regiment (the 88th or Connaught Rangers) and the 74th. Once they had grasped the situation they rose in revolt under a French emigré officer, the Chevalier de Liniers. Beresford was no genius, as his later generalship at Albuhera was to show, and he was heavily outnumbered. In the circumstances he did well to gain such favourable terms for his withdrawal. Popham could now do no more than await the reinforcements which he knew to be on the way.

That he should have been reinforced at all may seem, in the circumstances, surprising. But his first despatch, of 6th July, sent by the *Narcissus* and accompanied by over a million dollars, was an announcement of victory. He had occupied the capital " of one of the richest and most extensive provinces of South America." " To the commerce of Great Britain " he added, " it exhibits peculiar advantages, as well as to the active industry of her manufacturing towns." All that remained to do was to secure and defend a new possession. Characteristically, moreover, Sir Home Popham had written to the Mayor and Corporation of Birmingham by the same ship to inform them that " the conquest of this place opens an extensive channel for the manufactures of Great Britain." Hitherto, he points out, " the trade of this country has been cramped beyond belief . . . but from this moment its trade will be thrown open." As he had written on similar lines to the local authorities of the other manufacturing towns (in which his popularity was by now unbounded), a race for the new market had begun—a race in which one of Popham's relatives had something of a lead. If only to protect the trade, additional forces would have to go there. Whether Popham was to remain in command of them was, naturally, another matter.

Francisco Miranda, Popham's informant in South American affairs, had almost simultaneously led a private expedition to Venezuela. This failed, also for lack of local support, but not without causing a great sensation throughout South America. The events of 1806-7 proved to be an important step in the process by which the South American Provinces freed themselves from Spain.

8. Only complete success could have justified Sir Home Popham's action in proceeding to the River Plate and so quitting his proper station at the Cape. Initial success had turned to failure on 12th August and it was promptly decided, when the news reached England, to supersede him. Rear-Admiral Stirling was sent out with orders to send Popham home. The way in which he did this—acting either on his instructions or perhaps in accordance with a verbal hint— seemed, in effect, to pre-judge the verdict of the Court-Martial. His passage home in the unarmed *Rolla* was not dignified or even safe, and it is difficult to resist the conclusion that he was being persecuted as much for his politics as for his

failure. A Court-Martial decided on 11th March, 1807, that his proceeding to the River Plate was highly censurable, but "in consideration of circumstances" inflicted only a severe reprimand. Less than a month later a fresh change of administration brought in another Board of Admiralty with Admiral Gambier as the senior naval member. Sir Home Popham was at once employed again in positions of responsibility and lived to hoist his flag as Commander-in-Chief on the Jamaica Station in 1817-20.

9. John Whitelocke (1757-1833) was well-connected by marriage and had a reputation based mainly on his capture of the fort at Mole St. Nicholas in 1793, and his leadership of the attack on Port-au-Prince in 1794. His subsequent service had been as Lieut.-Governor of Portsmouth and Inspector-General of Recruiting. He reached Montevideo as Commander-in-Chief on 10th May, 1807, and decided (because of the season) not to await the further troops which would have brought his forces to a total of 11,000. Leaving 1,350 men at Montevideo, he attacked Buenos Ayres with 7,822 men and 16 guns. The garrison numbered 6,000, the population 70,000, and the town was unfortified save for barricades at the end of the streets. Still anxious to avoid alienating the colonists or damaging the town, Whitelocke sent in the attacking columns with their arms unloaded. His orders, which Walters quotes (See page 61) were not a model of lucidity, and he lost all control of the battle soon after it began. After Crauford's column, isolated, had been forced to surrender, De Liniers offered terms which Whitelocke was glad to accept. Court-martialled on reaching England, his trial lasted seven weeks. He pleaded that he had been led to suppose the inhabitants friendly from experiencing "the difference between the oppressive dominion of Spain and the benign and protecting government of his Majesty." It was shown, however, that he was "deficient in zeal, judgment and personal exertion," and he was accordingly cashiered.

The failure of these operations in the River Plate had results which ultimately helped the English exporters for whose benefit the stroke had been planned. The colonists were encouraged by their victory over England to risk a rebellion against Spain, and their economic isolation ended, in fact, during their brief period of English occupation. After

144

that experience of free trade, they were never at rest until their commercial freedom had been regained. Spain lost all control over the Argentine in 1810 and never, in fact, recovered it.

10. The Portuguese tried to appease the French until the last possible moment, even to the extent of breaking off relations with their English allies. It was only on discovering that this policy had failed in its object that the Prince of Brazil and the Royal Family embarked in the Portuguese fleet and joined Sir Sidney Smith's squadron off the Tagus on 29th November, 1807. The French troops were then only nine leagues distant. On 1st December Sir Sidney was able to report that the Royal Family of Braganza was proceeding to Brazil under his escort, there to continue the war and maintain the English Alliance.

"The Portuguese fleet," he wrote (eight sail of the line, four frigates, and smaller craft) "arranged itself under the protection of that of His Majesty, while the firing of a reciprocal salute of 21 guns announced the friendly meeting of those who but the day before were in open hostility, the Scene imprefsing every beholder except the French army on the hills, with the most lively emotion of gratitude to providence that there yet exists a Power in the world able as well as willing to protect the opprefsed, inclined to pardon the misguided, and capable by its fostering care to found new empires and alliances from the wreck of the old ones destroyed by the ephemeral power of the day, on the lasting basis of mutual interest."

11. Robert Corbet was commissioned in 1796, served on the coast of Egypt in 1801 and was promoted Commander in 1802. Lord Nelson thought highly of him and he was posted as Captain of the *Nereide* (36), in which he was present at the landings in the River Plate. In the same ship he was at the Cape and later at Bombay. There he incurred Sir Edward Pellew's displeasure by acting without orders as Senior Naval Officer; and it was there that his crew made complaints of his cruelty. He applied for a Court-Martial but Pellew could not form one at Bombay for lack of senior officers. He decided, therefore, to send the *Nereide* to the Cape; omitting, however, to explain to the crew what the position was. The sailors concluded that their complaints had been ignored, and a number of them mutinied

on the voyage to the Cape. On arrival there, the mutineers were tried by Court-Martial, ten of the ring-leaders being sentenced to death and one actually executed. In the Court-Martial which tried Captain Corbet himself, his cruelty was proved and, indeed, admitted. In his defence he pleaded the custom of the service and argued, in effect, that with a bad crew, cruelty was necessary. He was reprimanded. At Plymouth in 1810 the crew of the *Africaine* (38) mutinied on his appointment to that ship. He returned in her, however, to the Ile de France, where he was killed in action on 13th September, 1810.

12. Contemporary with Corbet and serving at the same time off the Ile de France was Captain Nesbit Willoughby (1777-1849), known as "the immortal" and noted for his cruelty, his reckless courage and his quarrelsome disposition. He was dismissed his ship as a Lieutenant and then dismissed the Service. Serving as a volunteer, he regained his rank and was promoted to command the *Otter* (18) and, later, the *Nereide*. At the time this extraordinary incident occurred the *Nereide*, Corbet's former ship, was under his command. He was as severe, perhaps, as his predecessor, but probably more capable. He was wounded and taken prisoner at Port Louis, having 222 casualties out of a crew of 281, and was subsequently retired on a pension. He employed his leisure by serving in the Russian army. Taken prisoner again, he was in the retreat from Moscow, but eventually escaped. He was a Rear-Admiral, and knighted, when he died.

THE END

INDEX

[All ships and vessels are under the heading "Ships"]

148

NOTES ON THE ILLUSTRATIONS

By Lieutenant S. WALTERS

Plate 1.—*Argo*, Commodore Bowen. Sam'l Walters, Mid. and Mate, April, 1798, to April 19th, 1802. *Monkey*, Lieuts. Weir and Tillard, cruising for smugglers.

Plate 2.—*Ville de Paris* for Spithead, having the Flag of Admiral the Honble Sir William Cornwallis, K.C.B., Vice-Admiral of Great Britain. Channel Fleet at a distance.

Plate 3.—H.M.S. *Raisonable*, appointed to her 9th March, 1805. Captain Robert Barton. Bearhaven, Ireland. Confirmed Lieut't to H.M. Ship *Goliath*, 8th March, 1805, Sir Charles Brisbane, K.C.B., Captain.

Plate 4.—At 6 p.m. Admiral Cornwallis's Fleet put to sea, Wind S.E. (*Impetueux* and *Goliath* in Torbay, Brixham and Barry Head seen). Dissolution of His Majesty's Ship *Venerable* 24th November, 1804. The same evening I was promoted from Mate of *Ville de Paris*. At 4 o'clock Sam Walters appointed by the above Admiral Acting Lieut. His Majesty's Ship *Goliath* (being next ship to the wreck). When the wind shifted from SW to SE, *Venerable*, casting the wrong way, (i.e. with her head inshore) —struck on a rock in Torbay as per date. The two ships above veer'd two cables and let go second anchor. Their boats, with great exertion—with the *Frisk* Cutter—saved all the crew. Lt. W. commanded the *Goliath's* Boats.

Plate 10.—12th November, 1812. A Sketch of H.M. Ship *Courageux* 74, Commodore Wilkinson, proceeding from the Baltic fleet to reinforce the squadron on the North American Station, selected by the Admiralty with H.M. Ship *Plantaganet*, being ships of the line having no poops, apparently like frigates. The latter mentioned ship having prudently anchored at Sunset, the former ship running after dark got on shore on the S.W. reef, Island of Anholt, and there remained near three hours, lost her rudder and very nearly met her dissolution, by which we were disappointed of trying our prowess with the United States men. S.W. 2nd Lieutenant at the time. A great misfortune to all, at that time considered so.

153

The drawings found unsuitable for reproduction comprise—

(*a*) A sketch of Cape La Havre Light houses and of its Port, with the Squadron under the command of Sir Rich'd Strachan, consisting of His Majesty's Ships *Diamond, Adamant, Niger* and *Argo*—the latter in the act of picking up a French Boat, on board of which Sir Sidney Smith had made his escape from France on the morning of the 4th May, 1798. By Samuel Walters, Mid. of the *Argo*.

(*b*) Table Bay, with Devil's Tongue, Table Mountain and Lion's Head.

(*c*) Sugar Loaf in the Harbour of Rio Janeiro, Brazil, Sth America, by Sretlaw Leumas, 13th Nov., 1813. From the vessel *Windham*.